Journe
TURKIS

Eric Teichman 342 30352

With an Introduction by Peter Hopkirk

HONG KONG
OXFORD UNIVERSITY PRESS
OXFORD   NEW YORK
1988

Oxford University Press

Oxford New York Toronto
Petaling Jaya Singapore Hong Kong Tokyo
Delhi Bombay Calcutta Madras Karachi
Nairobi Dar es Salaam Cape Town
Melbourne Auckland

and associated companies in
Berlin Ibadan

First published by Hodder and Stoughton Ltd., London, 1937
©Sir Eric Teichman 1937
Introduction © Oxford University Press 1988

This edition reprinted, with permission and with the
addition of an Introduction,
in Oxford Paperbacks 1988

ISBN 0 19 582711 2

Printed in Hong Kong by Golden Crown Printing Co. Ltd.
Published by Oxford University Press, Warwick House, Hong Kong

INTRODUCTION

IN the autumn of 1935, when Sir Eric Teichman drove westwards through Chinese Central Asia, most of this region was in the ruthless grip of a Stalinist puppet named Sheng Shi-tsai (Sheng Shi-cai), whose rule had effectively reduced it to being a Soviet colony in everything but name. Although the British had long had a Consulate-General which served as a listening-post at Kashgar (Kashi), they had no one at Urumchi (Urumqi), the provincial capital and Governor Sheng's head-quarters, and London was almost totally in the dark over what was going on there. It was the task of Teichman, a China-watcher of many years' experience, to try to find out on behalf of the mandarins at the Foreign Office precisely what was happening.

The virtual take-over of the Chinese province of Sinkiang (Xinjiang) by Stalin had come about some two years earlier, during the Christmas of 1933. It had followed a brutal holy war between the Tungans, or

Note: Place and personal names in the Introduction are spelled according to the Wade-Giles system of romanization, which is used in the main text of the book. Pinyin spelling is given in parentheses.

INTRODUCTION

Chinese Muslims, and the local Manchu authorities, which had lasted four dark and terrible years and had cost at least 100,000 lives. The Muslim insurgents were led by a formidable young war-lord named Ma Chung-yin (Ma Chong-Yin), known as General Ma — or sometimes, 'Big Horse'. Half bandit, half soldier, he was both a brilliant horseman and a crack shot, and possessed immense charisma. He was also an extremely capable soldier, and looked dangerously like realizing his dream of delivering his fellow Muslims from infidel Chinese rule and founding a great Islamic empire in Central Asia.

In January 1934, after being driven back twice before, Ma's troops, armed with long scaling ladders, and in greater force than ever, advanced once more on the walled city of Urumchi, confident that this time they would succeed in storming it. But unknown to Ma, much had happened during the intervening months, when he had been recovering from wounds. Worried lest Ma's insurrection should spill over the Sino-Soviet frontier and spread among his own Muslim Central Asian peoples, Stalin offered Governor Sheng the assistance of Red Army troops and aircraft in putting down the uprising. He was also worried about Ma's shadowy links with the Japanese, whose ambitions in the region were no secret. Sheng, who was being hard pressed by Ma and knew that his own government in Nanking (Nanjing) was in no position to help him, accepted the offer gratefully.

The Russian troops crossed into Sinkiang amid great secrecy as Ma was beginning his advance on Urumchi. Their arrival had to be kept secret not only from Ma, but also from Nanking, for Sheng had no authority to invite the Russians into China. One of the few Westerners in the area at that time, a young German airfield engineer named Georg Vasel, watched the Soviets arrive. It was a dangerous place for foreigners just then, and it was from a prison yard that he observed 'regiment after regiment' of Red Army troops marching through the snow towards Urumchi, accompanied by 'greyish-green monsters — armoured cars with machine-guns mounted on their steel turrets'. They were followed by a squadron of bombers, clearly Soviet, but with their markings removed.

The outcome was fairly predictable, both militarily and politically. Ma's troops, fanatically brave but poorly armed and ill-trained, were caught totally by surprise and driven back in disorder, fleeing westwards along the Silk Road towards Kashgar. Bombed, machine-gunned, and shelled, they lost some 2,000 men. Ma's broken army turned to banditry, while he himself withdrew to Kashgar, which he occupied with the troops who had remained loyal to him. Meanwhile the Soviets, who had sent in contingents of the OGPU with their troops, left the former behind while they withdrew the latter, whom they no longer needed to carry out their predatory designs on Sinkiang. With Sheng now their puppet, and their secret police now well entrenched, the province was virtually theirs, although nominally still governed, through Sheng, by China.

Meanwhile, in Kashgar, Ma had done a mysterious vanishing act. Without warning (only shortly before he had been observed playing tennis at the Swedish mission station), or explanation, he handed over command to his half-brother. Next day, travelling westwards into the Soviet Union on a Russian lorry, he left Sinkiang for ever. He was never seen again in these parts, although it was rumoured that he was living in exile in Moscow and was subsequently liquidated during the Stalin purges of the late 1930s. But quite why he should have put himself into the hands of those who had destroyed his dream will probably remain a mystery for ever.

INTRODUCTION

Meanwhile Urumchi and other parts of Sinkiang and neighbouring Kansu (Gansu) had been transformed into a Soviet-style police state. In addition to the unfortunate Vasel, a number of other foreigners were in jail there, among them the legendary George Hunter, a Christian missionary who had spent a lifetime in Chinese Central Asia. Sven Hedin, the celebrated Swedish explorer, was also detained, together with the rest of his expedition, but was allowed to go free, as eventually were Vasel and Hunter. Others were less fortunate, for thousands of innocent Chinese and Muslims were rounded up as suspects during the anti-Fascist witch-hunt that followed, and tortured, shot, or both.

By now British trade with Sinkiang, largely conducted through India, had shrunk to about a twentieth of what it had once been. This was the result of deliberate strangulation by Moscow, which was only too happy to replace these lost imports with Soviet-made goods, including cheap imitations of popular British products. At the same time life was made increasingly difficult for the British Consulate-General staff at Kashgar. It was at this moment that *The Times* of London decided to dispatch its special correspondent, Peter Fleming, to Sinkiang to try to establish the truth of the wild rumours circulating about what Sheng and his Russian friends were up to. However, he wisely avoided Urumchi — and the near certainty of sharing a cell there with Vasel — and with his travelling companion, Ella Maillart, decided instead to stick to the southern arm of the Silk Road, then still in the hands of the insurgents.

But although they both wrote entertaining accounts of their adventure — Fleming's *News from Tartary* (1936), and Maillart's *Forbidden Journey* (1937) — they were unable to discover at first hand what was happening in Stalin's grim satellite on the other side of the Taklamakan and Gobi deserts. None the less Fleming did discern Stalin's growing concern about Japanese aspirations in the region, and his consequent loss of interest in the task which had previously been Moscow's sworn intent, not to mention that of its Tsarist predecessors, namely, the undermining of British rule in British India.

This, then, was the arena into which Sir Eric Teichman rode in his somewhat ramshackle convoy of two lorries (one of which had belonged to Sven Hedin) not long after Fleming and Maillart had made their journey. But while they had steered well clear of Urumchi, Teichman headed straight for it, knowing that he not only enjoyed diplomatic immunity but also had the go-ahead from Nanking, which still nominally ruled Sinkiang. Even Stalin would be unlikely to want to provoke an incident with the British government by arresting, or otherwise harming, a senior British diplomat going about his lawful business. Indeed, as will be seen, Governor Sheng received Teichman warmly although he had earlier tried strenuously to prevent him from coming (in the interests of Teichman's own safety, as Sheng now hastily explained).

Born on 16 January 1884 (making him 51 at the time of this journey), Teichman was educated at Charterhouse and Cambridge, before entering the old Consular Service in 1907 as a student interpreter in Peking, where he was attached to the British Legation. He had served in China almost ever since, becoming Chinese Secretary, or chief adviser on Chinese affairs, to the Legation, and subsequently to the Embassy, in 1922. He spoke fluent Chinese, and few men knew more about the country than he did, since he had travelled in some of its most remote corners, including Kansu and Eastern Tibet (Xizang). These official journeys resulted in two books, *Travels*

INTRODUCTION

of a Consular Officer in North-West China (1921), and *Travels of a Consular Officer in Eastern Tibet* (1922), today both extremely rare. The first described journeys in Kansu and Shensi (Shaanxi) provinces made in connection with the Anglo-Chinese opium treaty, while the second dealt with a mission into regions contested by Chinese and Tibetan troops, between whom Teichman acted successfully as peacemaker.

Teichman was also a fine horseman and an expert polo player, but as a result of a serious fall he suffered from a bad stoop (visible in one or two of the many remarkable photographs in this book) which, curiously, did not show when he was in the saddle. In 1933 he received a knighthood for his long years of service in China, and his journey across Sinkiang (officially described as a mission) marked the final act of his career.

Teichman and his five-man party — two Mongols and three Chinese — set out for Urumchi on 18 September 1935. To say more about their journey, which was to carry them some 2,500 miles, via Hami (Qomul), Urumchi, Turfan (Tulufan), Kuchar (Kucha), and Aksu, to Kashgar, would be to spoil the author's own narrative. The book will be of particular interest to enthusiasts of pioneer motoring, or anyone wishing to emulate Teichman's journey, for it has a detailed itinerary, with notes on the particular difficulties of each stage. It also has an excellent folding map of the route, prepared from a compass traverse by the author.

The book will also contain much of interest for those who, in ever-increasing numbers, are crossing from Pakistan into Sinkiang via the Karakoram Highway. For in many places today's traveller can see the old route taken by all those who once passed between Gilgit and Kashgar clinging dizzily to the mountainside, with only just enough room for a pony to pass, and a terrifying drop of hundreds of feet below it if he stumbled. There are brief but interesting descriptions of Tashkurgan (Tash Qurghan), Gilmit, Baltit, and Gilgit, all of which are familiar to travellers using the Karakoram Highway today, half a century after Teichman passed that way.

Almost certainly on his return to Delhi or London Teichman wrote a detailed confidential report on the Soviet penetration of Sinkiang, and especially on the situation at Urumchi, where he spent some time. If so it is very likely to be found today in the secret archives of that period, either at the Public Records Office at Kew, or the India Office Library in London. But this I must leave to some enterprising reader to find, for I have yet to come upon it myself. However, in his Urumchi chapter, Teichman describes his talks with the ruthless Sheng, and his bibulous reception on Soviet National Day by the Russian Consul-General, the Governor's charming evil genius. In his final chapter the author outlines the political situation in Sinkiang as he saw it, or rather as his chiefs allowed him to portray it — for it was written long before the days of *Spycatcher*.

There remains one sad detail to be added. In December 1944, long after Teichman's retirement, he was walking one day in the grounds of his home in England when he disturbed a poacher. The intruder was a 28-year-old American serviceman from a nearby Air Force base. When challenged by Teichman, he raised his carbine and shot him dead. The man, said by the defence to have a mental age of nine, was found guilty of murder, flown back to the United States, and hanged.

Peter Hopkirk is the author of three books on the central Asian travellers: *Foreign Devils on the Silk Road*, *Trespassers on the Roof of the World*, and *Setting the East Ablaze*.

JOURNEY TO TURKISTAN

BY

SIR ERIC TEICHMAN
K.C.M.G., C.I.E.
OF HIS BRITANNIC MAJESTY'S CONSULAR SERVICE IN CHINA (RETIRED)

Author of " Travels in North-West China "
" Travels in Eastern Tibet "

LONDON
HODDER AND STOUGHTON LIMITED
St. Paul's House, London, E.C.4

PREFACE

In submitting to the public this account of my journey by motor truck through Mongolia and Chinese Turkistan I desire to acknowledge with gratitude the assistance and hospitality accorded to me by the following : Mr. George Soderbom of Suiyuan ; the *Tupan* and the Chinese and Turki authorities of Sinkiang ; Colonel and Mrs. Thomson Glover and the Consular Staff at Kashgar ; the Mir of Hunza ; Major and Mrs. Kirkbride of Gilgit ; and His Excellency the Viceroy and the Foreign and Political Department of the Government of India.

For the benefit of those who may have occasion to make a similar journey I have added in the form of an appendix an itinerary of the motor route from Peking to Kashgar.

CONTENTS

vii

CONTENTS

CHAPTER IV

CHAPTER V

CHAPTER VI

CHAPTER VII

CONTENTS

CHAPTER VIII

CHAPTER IX

CHAPTER X

CHAPTER XI

CONTENTS

CHAPTER XII

LIST OF ILLUSTRATIONS

*Where the photographs are not facing the page given they
are inside the set of photographs beginning on that page*

LIST OF ILLUSTRATIONS

LIST OF ILLUSTRATIONS

LIST OF ILLUSTRATIONS

CHAPTER I

INTRODUCTION

Features of Chinese Turkistan—Its peoples and recent
history—Mohammedan rebellions—Civil war between
Ma Chung-ying and the Chinese—Russian intervention
and defeat of Ma Chung-ying—Mission to Urumchi—
Relations between Urumchi and Nanking—Relations
with the U.S.S.R.—Difficulties in securing permission
to enter Sinkiang.

IN 1935 I was sent from China on a special mission
to Chinese Turkistan. Before telling the story of my
journey, I propose to devote this introductory chapter
to describing the circumstances in which it came to
be made. Firstly, a few paragraphs about Chinese
Turkistan, its features, peoples and recent history.
Readers who do not need to be instructed on such
points can skip these pages and start at Chapter II.

* * *

Sinkiang [1] is the dead heart of Central Asia, a
land of rainless deserts, oases and snow-fed streams
whose waters never reach the sea. It is crossed from
east to west by a great mountain range, aptly called
by the Chinese *T'ien Shan*, " Celestial Peaks," whose
snow-capped summits hang in the clear blue of the
North Asian skies above the dusty deserts far below
and greet the weary caravans from China as their
first landfall in Chinese Turkistan. The T'ien Shan

[1] Chinese Turkistan is known to the Chinese as *Sinkiang*,
which is the generally accepted rendering of the two Chinese
characters romanized according to the *Wade* system as *Hsin
Chiang* and meaning " The New Territory " or " New Dominion."

15

range divides the Province into two sections, North and South, Dzungaria and Eastern Turkistan.[1] The former is more Tartar, Mongol and Siberian in character ; the latter Turkish through and through.

The remoteness of Sinkiang is emphasized by its bad communications and the physical difficulties of reaching it from east or south. Coming from China the traveller has to cross a thousand miles of empty Gobi desert before reaching the borders of Chinese Turkistan ; while from India to Kashgaria one has for hundreds of miles to traverse the Himalaya, Karakoram and Pamir ranges by one of the most arduous mountain trails in the world. Communications with Russian Central Asia, on the other hand, are much easier, especially since the construction of the Turkistan-Siberian Railway, which connects the Trans-Caspian with the Trans-Siberian lines and provides rail communication near and all along the Russian frontier of Sinkiang.

* * *

The population of this desert land is naturally very sparse, perhaps three million, seventy per cent. or more of whom are Mussulmans of Turkish race. The bulk of these are *Turkis*, whom the Chinese call *Ch'an-t'ou*, or " Turban-heads," the agricultural inhabitants of the oases ; they are known to the Russians as *Sarts*, or, nowadays, *Uzbeks*. The rest of the Turkish Moslem population are made up of the *Kirghiz* and *Kazaks* (in Chinese *Hei-hei-tzu* and *Ha-sa*), who are the Mohammedan nomads of the uplands, the former in the south and the latter in the north

[1] The Chinese call the two parts of Sinkiang *T'ien Shan Pei Lu* and *T'ien Shan Nan Lu*, meaning the Circuits north and south of the T'ien Shan respectively.

Street Scene in Eastern Turkistan

Street Scene in Eastern Turkistan

On the South Road, Chinese Turkistan

On the South Road, Chinese Turkistan

of the Province, and other minor races, such as the *Tajiks* of the Pamir country in the South. All these peoples speak Turkish dialects and are of the same stocks as the corresponding races in Russian Central Asia, where the autonomous republics of Turkmanistan, Uzbekistan, Tajikistan, Kirghizstan and Kazakstan have been established as constituent parts of the U.S.S.R.

Side by side with these Turks there is a considerable population of Mongols, who, like all Mongols, are nomads and Buddhists of the Lama Church. The Mongols of Sinkiang (known to the Russians as Kalmucks) belong to the Torgut tribe which migrated in the seventeenth century to the Lower Volga region in Russia, where some of them are still found, and returned to Chinese Central Asia a hundred years later. They are now widely distributed on the upland pastures of the northern half of Sinkiang, while an outlying branch of the tribe occupies the Etsin Gol oasis in the Gobi, north of Kansu Province.

The third big element in the population of Sinkiang are the Chinese Moslems, known locally as *Tungans* (*T'ung-kan*), whose colonies extend from Shensi and Kansu (the latter Province being their main home) across Northern and Southern Sinkiang to Kashgar. These Tungans are the most war-like people amongst the native populations of Chinese Turkistan. In speech and culture they are Chinese, but they show in their appearance clear traces of a Central Asian origin.

The purely Chinese population of Sinkiang is relatively very small, consisting of soldiers and officials and a few merchants and colonists, the latter in the north of the Province. Especially nowadays, since the rebellion, a Chinese face is rarely seen in the crowded Turki bazaars south of the T'ien Shan.

* * *

Sinkiang has been in recent Chinese history the scene of devastating Mohammedan rebellions, the most formidable of which was the rising led by Yakub Beg, a soldier of fortune from Russian Central Asia, who, in the sixties and seventies of last century, set up an independent Moslem State in Chinese Turkistan. The Chinese Government of those days took their time, but in the end the rebellion was rigorously suppressed, the country reconquered and a new provincial administration introduced. Modern Sinkiang, "The New Dominion," dates from the eighties, when Yakub Beg's affair was finally cleared up. The last Mohammedan rebellion, until the recent troubles, occurred in 1895-6 amongst the Tungans of Kansu, then, as now, the danger-point of the north-west. Thereafter, Sinkiang and Kansu lay under the shadow of further rebellions ; but trouble was averted by the successful co-operation of the Chinese Government with the leaders of the Tungans, who enjoyed (and still enjoy in Kansu and the Kokonor) a large measure of autonomy, honours and high positions in the service of the State.

* * *

The recent troubles in Sinkiang began with the passing in 1928 of the old Governor Yang Tseng-hsin, who had ruled the Province since the revolution of 1911. During the time that Governor Yang was in control of Sinkiang, China Proper was passing through the troubles that attended the birth of the Chinese Republic, from the days of Yuan Shih-k'ai,

18

through the period of regional militarism which ensued on his death, down to the time of the Communist revolution in South China, the rise of the *Kuo-min-tang*,[1] and the establishment of the National Government at Nanking. During these two decades of turmoil in China, Yang Tseng-hsin was successful in preserving the old Imperial framework of administration, and with it law and order, in Sinkiang, and in keeping the New Dominion outside the factional politics of Republican China. He was, however, led by his own interests to exercise complete local autonomy and to pursue a policy of segregating Sinkiang from the rest of China. This was especially the case towards the end of his reign, when General Feng Yü-hsiang and the revolutionary *Kuo-min-chün*[2] were in control in North-West China. But if Governor Yang was suspicious of the new Nationalist movement in China Proper, he was equally anxious to keep revolutionary Russia at arm's length.

The assassination in 1928 of Yang Tseng-hsin ushered in a period of turmoil and revolution in Sinkiang. Under the rule of Governor Yang's successor, Chin Shu-jen, points of friction between the native population and the Chinese local government developed and increased. In 1930 the old Turki *Wang* (or Prince) of Hami, Shah Maksud, died and the Chinese authorities at Urumchi took steps to assume more direct control over the local administration of that region. This led in 1931 to a rising of the Hami Turkis against the Chinese. It happened that at this time there was a young Tungan General in Kansu named Ma Chung-ying, who had been

---

[1] "The National People's Party," the ruling party in China.

[2] "The National People's Army," the name given by General Feng to his troops.

fighting to maintain himself against Feng Yü-hsiang and the *Kuo-min-chün* in North-West China. He joined his co-religionists, the Mohammedan rebels of Hami, and led his army of Kansu Tungans into Sinkiang against the Chinese.

Hostilities between Ma Chung-ying and the Chinese authorities in Urumchi ebbed and flowed across the plains of Northern Sinkiang for the next two years. In the spring of 1933 developments occurred which led to the defeat of the Tungans. The Chinese at Urumchi, who had with difficulty been holding their own, assisted by a force of local Russian mercenaries, were opportunely reinforced by the arrival in Sinkiang from Siberia of a strong body of Chinese troops expelled by the Japanese from Manchuria in the previous year. At the same time the Governor, Chin Shu-jen, was overthrown by a local *coup*, and was succeeded by the present ruler of the province, General Sheng Shih-ts'ai, a Manchurian officer of the Chinese General Staff who had been sent to Sinkiang in a military capacity a year or two before. General Sheng, a younger and more forceful figure than his predecessor, carried on the war against Ma Chung-ying. He was greatly strengthened by the Chinese reinforcements from Manchuria, but the decisive factor which enabled him to defeat the Tungans was the assistance of the Russian authorities, with whom he reached an understanding and who decided at this juncture to throw their weight in the scale on the side of the Chinese. Before the end of the year this Russian intervention in Northern Sinkiang had proved decisive and Ma Chung-ying withdrew with his army to the south of the province.

In the meantime the troubles had spread to Southern Sinkiang, where the local Turkis and Kirghiz, combining with the Tungans, had risen against and swept away the local Chinese administration in Kashgaria. In the early summer of 1933, however, the Turkis and Tungans fell out and for the rest of the year a Turki régime was in control at Kashgar, with the local Tungan force besieged in the New City, the Chinese citadel six miles out from the old town of Kashgar. Early in 1934, the civil war having gone against the Tungans in the north, Ma Chung-ying, withdrawing down the South Road, arrived in Kashgar, where he relieved the besieged Tungan garrison, overthrew the native Turki régime and took over control of the local government. The Tungan ascendancy in Kashgaria was, however, short-lived. In July, 1934, General Sheng's provincial troops, represented by a combined force of Manchurians and Turkis, reached Kashgar and drove out the Tungans, who withdrew without fighting to Yarkand and Khotan. Ma Chung-ying himself caused general surprise by fleeing across the border into Russian Central Asia.

*　　*　　*

By the year 1935 active hostilities between the Chinese and the Tungans had ceased and Sinkiang was settling down under the rule of General Sheng Shih-ts'ai, who was in effective control of the whole province with the exception of the Khotan area still occupied by the Tungans in the south. It was at this juncture that the British Government decided to send a special mission to Urumchi to establish contact with the new régime and discuss with the local Government outstanding questions and measures for the restoration of British and Indian trade. British interests in Sinkiang concern trade with India and the activities of Indian traders in Turkistan, the peace of the North-West Frontier, and the British trade, such as it is, which penetrates to Chinese Central Asia from the China coast. We are permanently represented in Sinkiang by a Consul-General (at that time Colonel J. W. Thomson Glover, C.B.E.), appointed from the Indian Service and residing at Kashgar, which is nearly a thousand miles from Urumchi, the provincial capital. The plan was that Colonel Thomson Glover should travel up from his post to Urumchi, while I, coming from our Embassy in China (of which nominally Sinkiang is but a province), journeyed overland to meet him there. We were then, after our discussions with the local Government, to return together to Kashgar, whence I would make my way through India home. This plan was successfully accomplished. Leaving Peking on September 14, I arrived in Delhi exactly four months later. The last part of the journey was a race against time ; for from November on the passes into India are generally closed by snow till May or June. I seemed, therefore, to be booked to spend the winter in Chinese Turkistan. But, spurred on by the prospect of reaching England by the spring, I hustled through and scrambled over the Pamir and Karakoram in midwinter, finishing my journey, by courtesy of the Government of India, by aeroplane across the Himalaya. I had started the journey by train, from Peking to Suiyuan on the Chinese Mongolian border ; covered the next 2,500 miles through Mongolia and Turkistan by motor truck ; continued from Kashgar to Gilgit, 400 miles, by pony and on foot ; and finished the journey from Gilgit to Delhi by air.

*   *   *

Turn up the map of Asia and you will see the line of my motor route, north of latitude 40, from Peking, through Inner Mongolia and across the Gobi Desert to Hami, and thence through the length of Chinese Turkistan to Urumchi and Kashgar.

* * *

The relations between Urumchi and Nanking were at this time unfortunately far from what they should have been between a Provincial and a Central Government. General Sheng and the Government at Urumchi professed their loyalty and obedience to the National Government of China at Nanking. But in practice they enjoyed complete autonomy and did not allow the latter to do more than exercise a measure of influence in Sinkiang. This state of affairs, which is not unknown in other outlying parts of the Chinese Republic, and which, in the absence of foreign complications, would not need to provoke any particular attention, had arisen from the historical and geographical circumstances of the case. As indicated in a previous paragraph, the former Governor Yang Tseng-hsin, while showing no secessionist tendencies, segregated Sinkiang from China Proper and ruled the province for seventeen years with very little reference to the Central Government then located in Peking. Since the death of Governor Yang circumstances had tended to increase the estrangement between Urumchi and Nanking. For four years the Chinese provincial authorities of Sinkiang were engaged in a life-and-death struggle with the Tungans. The Central Government, not being in a position to intervene, adopted a neutral wait-and-see attitude towards both parties in this struggle ; the " Pacification Commissioners," General Huang Mu-sung and

Dr. Lo Wen-kan, whom they sent to Sinkiang in 1933, met with less than no success ; and mutual misunderstandings and suspicions between Nanking and Urumchi were bound to arise. General Sheng and his colleagues had thus been led to continue and accentuate the policy of their predecessors of isolating the New Dominion from the rest of China. No one, whether Chinese or foreigner, could enter Sinkiang without the permission of Urumchi, and it had in many cases been found even more difficult to get out of the province.

The local corollary of strained relation with China was a closer intimacy with the U.S.S.R. For geographical and racial reasons the connection between Chinese Turkistan and the neighbouring territories of Siberia and Russian Central Asia must always, unless artificially suspended for political reasons, be specially close and intimate. The native peoples of Turkistan, the Turkis, Tajiks, Kirghiz and Kazaks, are of the same stocks and speak the same Turkish dialects on both sides of the border. Moreover, owing to its situation, Sinkiang, which looks out onto Russian Central Asia and turns its back on China, is economically dependent on the U.S.S.R. And it is inevitable that such economic dependence should be accompanied by a measure of political influence, an influence which has been greatly strengthened by the events of recent years and the assistance rendered by the Russians to the Chinese authorities at Urumchi in their struggles with Ma Chung-ying.

These conditions in the internal politics of Chinese Turkistan were not without their complications for my mission. The decision to send me to Sinkiang was reached in the early summer of 1935, when the Chinese Government were approached and requested to facilitate my journey. This they readily agreed to do ; but, on applying to General Sheng and his administration at Urumchi for facilities on my behalf, they received evasive and unsatisfactory replies, politely veiling a refusal to receive me. Local political conditions were said to be unfavourable ; there had been an outbreak of plague in Southern Turkistan, unrest and brigandage rendered the roads unsafe for travellers and it would be difficult to afford protection. For many weeks the question of my mission was argued in a desultory wireless correspondence between Urumchi and Nanking. But finally, in August, when the whole project seemed to have faded into nothingness, the authorities in Chinese Turkistan shifted their ground and agreed, if we insisted on the journey being made, to do their best to facilitate my mission and afford protection on the road.

Whatever may have been behind these obscure negotiations and delays, permission for me to enter Turkistan was thus obtained ; and, when I eventually crossed the border and entered Sinkiang, I and my party, and Colonel Thomson Glover and his staff, were overwhelmed with kindness and hospitality from first to last.

* * *

When I got home I lectured to my fellow members of the Royal Central Asian Society on *Chinese Turkistan*, and to those of the Royal Geographical Society on *The Motor Route from Peking to Kashgar*. Later I received several inquiries from travellers contemplating a similar motor tour to Turkistan ; and one evening not long since I was rung up on the telephone by a lady who was leaving for China the next day and who asked me for all the necessary information about how to motor from Peking to Kashgar. While flattered that my lectures should have aroused this interest, I should like to add a post-script *caveat*— namely, that, while the physical difficulties in the way of such a journey can with due preparation easily be overcome, the political obstacles are more formidable and may prove insuperable at the present time.

CHAPTER II

PREPARATION

Routes to Sinkiang—Possibilities of motor transport—
George Soderbom—Political difficulties—By train to
Suiyuan—Preparations for the expedition—Equipment
and supplies—Personnel of the expedition—Our motor
transport—Cost of the journey—General Fu Tso-yi,
Governor of Suiyuan—Arms for self-defence—The Sin-
sui motor company—News of Gustav Soderbom's
release.

THE decision having been reached to send me to
Sinkiang, the question arose as to how I was to get
there. Urumchi can be reached from three direc-
tions ; from Kashmir in India across the Himalaya,
Karakoram and Pamir to Kashgar, and thence a
further journey of near a thousand miles through
Eastern Turkistan to Urumchi ; from China across
the Gobi desert to Hami and thence on across the
T'ien Shan range to Urumchi ; and *via* the Trans-
Siberian and Turkistan-Siberian railways through
Russian Central Asia to the Chinese frontier town of
Chuguchak (Ta-ch'eng) and thence by cart or motor
truck across the Dzungarian steppe to Urumchi. Of
the three routes that *via* Russia is the shortest and
easiest, provided the necessary permits and facilities
are obtainable from the authorities of the U.S.S.R. ;
and, were conditions more normal in this rather
abnormal part of the World, no one in their senses
bound for Urumchi would travel any other way.
There is not much to choose between the Indian
and Chinese routes, the former involving weeks of
travel with pack animals across the roof of Asia and

27

the latter a weary journey across the Gobi desert before the frontiers of Sinkiang are reached. In my case, travelling under Chinese auspices from the Chinese side, it was preferable to make the journey through Chinese territory and enter Sinkiang by the Gobi route.

* * *

For a brief period a few years ago one could actually fly from Shanghai to Urumchi in the machines of the Eurasia Air Line. This enterprising Sino-German concern intended originally to open an air service from Peking, across Mongolia, Siberia and Russia to Berlin. Trouble with the Outer Mongols, who shot down one of the machines, put a stop to this plan, and the Eurasia Company sought an alternative route to Europe across Sinkiang and Central Asia. They made several successful flights to Urumchi, but the Mohammedan rebellion intervened and the political difficulties soon became aggravated to the point of compelling the abandonment of the enterprise. In 1935 the Eurasia machines were flying regularly to Ninghsia and Lanchow in Kansu, but not beyond.

* * *

There are three main trails leading from China to Urumchi; the old Imperial road, a cart track, through Shensi and Kansu, which in 1935 was closed by the red armies operating in North-Western China; the old main caravan road through Outer Mongolia and along the southern base of the Altai mountains, which is no longer practicable from China owing to the closure of the Outer Mongolian frontier; and the small camel road, lying between the two, through

28

Inner Mongolia and across the Black Gobi to Hami. The latter route has, of recent years, come into more general use owing to the abandonment of the main camel trail through Outer Mongolia. It traverses between Suiyuan (Kwei-hwa-ch'eng) and Hami the whole length of the Gobi for a thousand miles, and is therefore the most arduous, but also politically the most peaceful, of the three roads ; and, as the Kansu trail was closed it was in any case for me the only open route.

*   *   *

From the outset I had been determined to try out the possibilities of motor transport ; which alone would enable me, starting in the autumn, to complete my mission and get through to India before the passes closed. I knew that the journey across the Gobi to Hami by motor had been successfully accomplished a few years before by a party of China Inland missionaries bound for Urumchi, by the Hardt-Citroen motor-tractor expedition in 1932, and by Sven Hedin in 1934 ; while an enterprising Chinese concern called the Sin-sui (Sinkiang Suiyuan) Motor Transportation Company were actually running occasional caravans of motor trucks between Suiyuan and Hami. I found it, however, difficult to obtain any definite information about the possibilities of getting through to Kashgar, beyond the fact that various big rivers, especially those at Karashar and Aksu, were likely to prove insurmountable obstacles. Actually I found when I got into Sinkiang that Russian *Amo* motor trucks were frequently driven through from Urumchi to Kashgar and that this part of the route was on the whole an easier proposition for motor traffic than the crossing of the Gobi desert.

My preliminary difficulties resolved themselves from the time that I got into touch with George Soderbom, a member of a Swedish missionary family well known on the Mongolian border, who was established as a trader at Kwei-hwa-ch'eng, the Chinese frontier town, now called Suiyuan, on the Peking–Suiyuan railway. George Soderbom had returned in the spring of the same year, 1935, from Sven Hedin's adventurous motor expedition to Chinese Turkistan and I was fortunate in being able to place all the preparations for my journey in his capable hands. These preparations concerned the purchase of two motor trucks, with spare parts and special equipment for extricating them from sand and mud, including special jacks, picks and spades, wire towing hawsers, planks and mats of rope ; the dispatch of a caravan of camels to lay down supplies of petrol in the desert for use *en route* ; and the selection of food supplies, Mongol tents, felts, sheepskins, and the many articles of native equipment necessary for such a journey.

* * *

I had originally fixed my departure for the end of September, but, as the days of preparation passed, it remained a question whether we should be able to get started at all. As so often happens when one contemplates a journey of this kind through China nowadays, reports and rumours of wars, rebellions, disturbances and outbreaks of brigandage succeeded one another almost from day to day. The Chinese communists had broken out afresh in Shensi and Kansu and threatened to spread northwards into Inner Mongolia and close the Gobi route ; bandits were on the war-path along the Suiyuan and Ninghsia borders, a region where brigandage is always rife ;

the Japanese were exerting increased pressure in Eastern Inner Mongolia, which had been closed to foreign travellers after the murder in the summer of a British journalist on the Chahar-Manchurian border ; and finally the news arrived of trouble in Suiyuan territory with a recalcitrant Mongol Prince, who had fallen foul of the newly established Inner Mongol Political Council and threatened to start a small war of his own in the region of Inner Mongolia through which I was to pass. In these circumstances I decided, although my petrol camels had not yet had enough start to reach their farthest destination in time, to hurry off and try and get through the inhabited regions of Inner Mongolia and out into the empty Gobi desert before further developments intervened and prevented my getting started at all.

* * *

The traveller's jumping-off place for a Gobi journey into the north-west is either Suiyuan or Kalgan, according to the prevalence of brigandage and the political circumstances of the moment. In my case it was Suiyuan or nowhere, since Chahar, the country north of Kalgan, was closed to foreign travel. It is physically possible to start for Central Asia by motor truck from the gates of Peking. But by taking advantage of the Peking-Suiyuan railway and starting from Suiyuan one is saved the difficult motor trip through the Nankow Pass and three to four hundred miles of bad going along the Inner Mongolian border.

I left Peking by train on September 14 and arrived the next morning at Suiyuan, where I spent some days in the hospitable Swedish home of Mr. and Mrs. Oberg, while making, with George Soderbom's assistance, the final preparations for the start. The sun shone and the dust blew in the brilliantly fine North China autumn weather, while Mongols, Chinese, camels and motor trucks jostled one another in the yard of the Oberg home, which was congested with tents, petrol drums, piles of food and kitchen and other camp equipment. One day was spent in sewing the felt on the insides of the Mongol tents, of which we had three, one for me and two for kitchen and staff. These are the best tents for travel in the north-west, light, easily pitched and folded, and, owing to the cut of the cotton cloth which pulls out at each end, remarkably roomy for their size. Lined with felt for winter travel, they make a snug retreat against the cold ; and, low and squat on the ground, they can withstand, better than a more upright tent, the great winds that blow across Mongolia.

Another day was occupied with the Chinese tailors and outfitters of Suiyuan who made up our equipment of felts and sheepskins. Each man was provided with a sleeping-felt, a pair of felt Mongol knee-boots, a cap of felt and fur, and sheepskin trousers, jacket, robe and sleeping-bag. With the exception of the last named, for the introduction of which the foreigner can claim the credit, the above is the camel-puller's outfit, which, if the cut of the skin coat and trousers is not altogether in the latest Peking fashion, affords the best possible protection against the cold. The Suiyuan sheepskins are amongst the best in Asia and superior to anything of the kind obtainable in Sinkiang or on the Indian frontier. Only the Mongolian wolfskin makes a warmer coat.

Many years' experience of travel in China, Tibet, Mongolia and Turkistan have taught me that in nine cases out of ten the native article of equipment is the best. One might spend much money in purchas-

Trying out the Mongol Tents in Suiyuan

Desert Camp

Lü Chen-lin, Serat and Liu Kuo-yi

Photo by Serat and Kuo Shu-ming

Lü Chen-lin, a Turki Soldier, Chomcha and Kuo Shu-ming

Photo by Serat and Kuo Shu-ming

ing the most expensive tents and wind- and cold-proof clothing that the outfitters and tailors of Europe can supply and not be as well off in the cold of a Mongolian winter as one would be with the tents, felts and sheepskins of native make.

The same principle applies to food supplies and in the long run one will fare better on fresh native produce than on the most expensive tinned foods. Apart from a few indispensable stores such as tea, coffee, sugar, jam, butter, tinned milk, cooking fat, salt, baking powder, soup sticks, matches, candles and soap, our supplies comprised mainly sacks of local flour, potatoes, onions and other vegetables, native condiments and dried fruits. Nothing but mutton, game shot on the road, and occasionally milk and butter, can be obtained *en route* during the journey of 1,200 miles through Mongolia and across the Gobi desert to Hami, the first oasis in Chinese Turkistan.

*   *   *

It is time I introduced the personnel of the expedition, comprising, as well as myself, two Mongols and three Chinese. First and foremost there was Serat (more correctly *Cerot*, but he has been immortalized in Sven Hedin's books under the former spelling, so let it stand). Serat, a Chahar Mongol, originally in the service of Mr. Larson, had accompanied Dr. Hedin on both his 1928 and 1934 expeditions to Sinkiang, on the former as a camel man and on the latter as motor-truck driver. When first approached on the subject of another journey to Sinkiang, Serat looked very glum and intimated that nothing would induce him, after his experiences with Sven Hedin on the latter's last trip to Chinese Turkistan,[1] to

[1] See *Big Horse's Flight*, by Sven Hedin.

3

venture there again. But eventually he agreed to go, on my undertaking to see him safely out of the country again *via* India. His services proved invaluable and he was my right-hand man from the day we left Suiyuan in our motor trucks to that on which we rode into Gilgit on our Turki ponies. I doubt if there is anyone living with a greater knowledge of the routes and practical details of motor travel in Mongolia and Chinese Turkistan; and I found him as expert in dealing with the mechanism of a Ford truck as he was in the management of camels and ponies and all the details of caravan and camp.

Next to Serat in importance came Chomcha, another Chahar Mongol trained by the Swedes as motor driver and mechanic. Like Serat, Chomcha had driven one of the trucks on Sven Hedin's last expedition. He looked to Serat for leadership, but was a cheerful lad, a careful driver and an excellent mechanic. Chomcha also knew something about bandaging and first aid, and served as well as barber to the party.

Of the three Chinese, Kuo Shu-ming, a first-class driver and mechanic, had been my chauffeur in Peking for fifteen years since his return from service with the Chinese Labour Corps in France. Kuo acted as relief driver to Chomcha, and, being able to read and write Chinese, was also useful as secretary and accountant to the expedition. Lü Chen-lin, another Pekinese, was my " boy," or personal servant. Liu Kuo-yi, the cook, was a Suiyuan man, trained by the Swedish missionaries and accustomed to desert travel on the Mongolian border. His cuisine was limited but adequate, and I lived very well throughout the journey. The Chinese have a racial genius for cookery; and the Chinese cook, and especially one accustomed to camp life, can produce amazingly good, if simple, meals in the most difficult and unpromising circumstances. We also had with us two additional hands recruited locally and not entered on our passport, one a Chinese from Kansu named Liu Chia, who had been with Sven Hedin's last expedition, and a Mongol named Göling, who returned from Hami. The whole party were, as an American-speaking young Chinese described them, " a pretty good group." Serat, a pessimist by nature, always expected and foretold the worst and invariably made the best of everything. None of them gave any trouble and all served me loyally and well and proved their worth when things were going wrong.

*　　*　　*

Our transport comprised two Ford V8 trucks, with special bodies built in Tientsin for expedition work after the model used by Sven Hedin. One was new and cost the equivalent of £237 in Peking. The other was a second-hand truck which I took over in Suiyuan for £150 from George Soderbom, who had inherited it from Dr. Hedin's expedition. It was in fact the truck presented by Mr. Edsel Ford to Sven Hedin, the adventures of which are so graphically related in Dr. Hedin's book about his last expedition. Truck *Edsel*, as it was named, let us down, suffering three major mechanical collapses and having finally to be abandoned in the deserts of Eastern Turkistan. The new truck, on the other hand, apart from one front spring which had to be changed, arrived in Kashgar after its journey of 2,500 miles from Suiyuan in perfect condition without having suffered as much as a puncture *en route*. The moral to be drawn from our experience in this respect was that one cannot beat the Ford V8 truck for expedition work but that it is foolish to trust to anything but new machinery for a journey of this kind. A major breakdown in the middle of the desert is a serious matter and may lead to a catastrophe ; and the stresses and strains of Gobi travel and the nature of some of the ground that has to be traversed must be seen to be believed. *Edsel* had been through it all the year before and its constitution just could not stand the strain again.

In its financial aspects the cost of a motor journey to Sinkiang depends on the condition in which one's truck arrives at its destination and on one's ability to dispose of it there on favourable terms. A new truck arriving in good condition is worth more in Urumchi or Kashgar than its prime cost in Peking or Tientsin ; so that with ordinary luck the cost of the journey should be confined to expenditure on petrol and oil and the ordinary expenses of the road. There may, however, be some difficulty in disposing of one's truck, as motor transport in Sinkiang is monopolized by the local Government. In my case our surviving truck was taken over by His Majesty's Consul-General in Kashgar at cost price. The cost to Government (salaries and allowances apart) of my journey to Kashgar amounted therefore to the purchase price of *Edsel*, plus the cost of petrol, oil, food supplies and equipment. It was not an expensive journey, and, had *Edsel* not crocked up, it would have been a very cheap one.

* * *

During our stay in Suiyuan we were all entertained by General Fu Tso-yi, the Governor of Suiyuan Province. General Fu is a Shansi man, whose good

The Start

Group of the Expedition Staff at a Gobi Well

Our Two Trucks in the Gobi

Camel Transport

reputation has survived the ins-and-outs of military and political life in North China during the turmoil of the past ten years. He had been informed of my mission by the Chinese Government, and when I asked him whether conditions on my route were peaceful and what my prospects were of reaching Sinkiang in safety, he refrained from committing himself beyond expressing the cautious opinion that it depended on my reception by the authorities of Chinese Turkistan. I had rather expected him to send an escort of soldiers with me to the borders of his territory, which might have raised awkward questions of transport. But he did not do so, and we travelled unescorted for the first 1,200 miles of our journey from Suiyuan to Hami.

I had given a good deal of thought to this question of protection and self-defence, which is nowadays a difficult and complicated one for the traveller in Chinese territory. When I first went out to China thirty years ago, one could travel over the length and breadth of the Chinese Empire in complete safety, unarmed and escorted by a magistrate's runner, equipped probably with nothing more formidable than a fan and umbrella. Then came the revolution of 1911, followed by the long era of civil wars, the growth of banditry and the general breakdown of law and order, aggravated of recent years by the depredations of the red armies ; so that the foreign traveller in the interior of the Chinese Republic is nowadays a danger to himself and a source of trouble and anxiety to his own and the Chinese authorities. The use of firearms for self-protection is also a doubtful proposition. Their use *may* put the aggressors to flight, but may also precipitate a tragedy or lead to embarrassing consequences ; seeing that the dividing line between soldiers, rebels and bandits is sometimes a vanishing one. Our armament, apart from my sporting shot-gun, comprised three revolvers, which we carried in a haversack so as to be handy in the cab of my truck. We never used them, except for occasional revolver practice for all hands in camp, the results of which appeared to indicate that we should have been at least as big a danger in a battle to ourselves as to the enemy.

* * *

I was also able, during our stay in Suiyuan, to make contact with the local manager of the Sin-sui (Sinkiang Suiyuan) Motor Transportation Company. This enterprising Chinese concern owned a fleet of motor trucks with which they maintained an intermittent service between Suiyuan and Hami. They would have been glad to run through to Urumchi and Kashgar ; but the Urumchi Government, in accordance with their traditional policy of exclusion, would not permit the Sin-sui trucks to run beyond Hami. Moreover, every Hami-bound passenger had to get permission from Urumchi to enter Sinkiang before starting from Suiyuan ; while it was equally, and sometimes more, difficult to secure permits to leave than to enter the province. In these conditions the trade of the Sin-sui trucks could hardly be a flourishing one. Actually they were at this time doing fairly well on the outward run in conveying to Hami the families and effects of the Manchurian soldiery in Sinkiang. But they were returning practically empty. With ordinary luck, the 1,200 miles from the China border to Hami can be covered by motor truck in two to three weeks, as against the two to three months occupied on the same journey by camel caravan or cart. The Chinese and their goods are always on the move, and there are no people on earth readier to appreciate and take advantage of modern methods of transportation, as one can often see illustrated by the hordes of passengers packed like flies in and around any Chinese country train or motor-bus ; and, were political conditions in Sinkiang more favourable, it is safe to assume that the Sin-sui Company would be reaping a golden harvest and their trucks loaded to full capacity on every trip each way. With the Japanese and their Mongol and Manchurian adherents pressing in from the east and Soviet influence barring the way to the west, the Sin-sui Company have a hard row to hoe. I hope they may yet make good. They certainly deserve full marks for their courage and enterprise in seeking to conquer the sands of the Gobi in the face of so many natural and artificial obstacles.

*   *   *

The evening before we were due to start from Suiyuan George Soderbom received a telegram conveying the good news that his brother Gustav, who had been detained for three years in Urumchi, had been released from prison and was on his way down from Hami with a convoy of Sin-sui trucks. Gustav Soderbom, whom I had last met some years earlier in happier circumstances on the Peking racecourse, was one of the pioneers of the motor route to Sinkiang, if he was not actually the first to drive through *via* the Black Gobi and the Etsin Gol. Several unsuccessful attempts had been made to drive a motor vehicle across the Inner Mongolian Gobi when some five years ago Gustav, having purchased a decrepit Cadillac car from a retiring American Minister in

Peking, set out from Suiyuan with Serat to try and get through to Hami. The main obstacle had always been the belt of sand, impassable to motor traffic, which stretches from the Kansu border through the Alashan desert northwards across Inner Mongolia to the Outer Mongolian frontier. On this occasion Gustav Soderbom and Serat solved the problem of these sands by making a dash through Outer Mongolia, when they had to " step on the gas " to avoid the Outer Mongol patrols. This was a risky adventure, but they got away with it and reached Hami in safety. On their return journey they discovered a way through the sands along, but on the right side of, the Outer Mongolian border. This is the trail since successfully followed by other expeditions and now in process of being developed into a regular motor route from China to Turkistan. Later on Gustav made another journey to Urumchi with motor trucks ordered by the then Governor of Sinkiang. It was at this time that the Mohammedan rebellion and civil warfare in Sinkiang broke out, with results involving in some way the affairs of Gustav Soderbom, who had suffered years of detention in Chinese Turkistan. The prisons of Urumchi are places of sinister repute and all the efforts so far made to effect the release of Gustav had been without avail. George was therefore much elated by the good news of his brother's escape and announced his intention of accompanying us on the following day to Pai-ling Miao, where the Sin-sui convoy and Gustav were due shortly to arrive.

CHAPTER III

THE SANDS OF THE GOBI :
FROM SUIYUAN TO THE ETSIN GOL

The start from Suiyuan—Mongolian grasslands—Pai-
ling Miao Monastery—Mr. Gonzell—The Autonomous
Government of Inner Mongolia—Arrival of Gustav
Soderbom—Across the prairies west from Pai-ling
Miao—Uni-ussu and the beginning of the Gobi—Life
of the camel trails—Shantan Miao Monastery and the
Winding Road—The Meringen Gol and the sandhills
of Bayen Unter—Rain and trouble with soft ground—
Bogged trucks—Hoyer Amatu—Breakdown in the
desert—Water shortage—Camp in Outer Mon-
golia—Bandin Tologoi and Borodin's road to Urga—
Arrival at the Etsin Gol.

ON the eighteenth of September, 1935, we lumbered
out through the dusty streets of Suiyuan bound for
Kashgar, the two trucks piled high with petrol drums,
luggage, stores, tents and equipment. Serat and I
drove in the cab of one truck, Chomcha and Kuo in
that of the other, while the rest of the party were
perched precariously, but not uncomfortably, on the
top of the loads. Each truck carried a load of about
three tons, including 320 gallons of petrol, sufficient,
at an estimated maximum consumption of four miles
to the gallon per truck, to take us at least six hundred
and forty miles on the way to Turkistan. Climbing
up through the stony pass, which leads from Suiyuan
and China out onto the Mongolian plateau, we met
with our first minor mishap, when a rock became
wedged in the dual rear wheels of one of the trucks
and took half an hour to dislodge. Curiously enough,
this particular kind of trouble only occurred once

again on the whole journey. In a gloomy gorge in the pass my wife, who had come thus far to see me off, turned back. We wondered whether, where and when we should meet again.

Beyond the pass we careered across the Mongolian prairie, the open rolling country-side of great distances which, from near the Pacific to Central Asia, lies everywhere behind the mountains of China's north-west frontier. I took my turn at the wheel, and we spun along with the eight-cylinder engine pulling its heavy load as smoothly as a saloon car. I had travelled many thousands of miles through the interior of China and her borderlands, but never before in such comfort and at such a pace. Our motor journey to Central Asia seemed a simple and pleasant affair : but disillusion was to follow.

We should have made the hundred miles to Pai-ling Miao in one day. But the first start is always a late one, and by nightfall we had only covered half the distance, reaching a stream called Chao Ho (Shara-muren), where we pitched our Mongol tents and made the first of many camps. Near by were a small monastery and a Chinese fort. On the following morning a half-day's run across the grassy steppe brought us to Pai-ling Miao, one of the biggest monasteries in Mongolia. Pai-ling Miao is the Chinese name ; the Mongols call it Batur Halak.

* * *

As in Tibet, these big Mongol monasteries present a startling sight in the otherwise empty land, where one may travel for days and weeks without seeing a tree or building of any kind. They stand as mighty monuments to the power of the Lama Church. The monastery of Pai-ling Miao lies backed by low hills in a grassy valley above a sandy stream. Near by, across the stream, is a busy Chinese bazaar ; for Pai-ling Miao is also the grassland terminus for the Gobi caravans, whose camels rest and recuperate on the pastures round about. Alongside the monastery there clustered, like monstrous pimples on the open plain, a groups of yurts [1] which housed the newly created " Autonomous Government of Inner Mongolia." [2]

Leaving the monastery on our left across the stream, we drove to the yurts of Mr. Gonzell, of the American Scandinavian Mission, the last outpost of the White Man on the road to Turkistan. We were soon eating a good lunch, which included a dish of stewed wild rhubarb from the hills. Gonzell had thrown down his challenge to the lamas by boldly establishing himself under the very walls of the great monastery. But the Mongol, while ready enough to take advantage of the medical services of the foreign missionary, is as little responsive to his teaching as the people of Tibet. It requires something more than the efforts of isolated Christian missionaries to break the power of the Lama Church (as it has, for instance, been broken in Outer Mongolia). But one could not fail to be impressed by Gonzell's single-minded zeal and earnestness of purpose ; and, if he had few converts, he seemed to have many friends and patients amongst the local Mongols.

In the afternoon, accompanied by George Soderbom, I went across to call on the Autonomous Government of Inner Mongolia, housed in their small and rather dirty looking yurts alongside the monastery.

[1] The circular felt tents of the Mongols.
[2] See note on page 66.

The head of the Government, Prince Tê,[1] the leader of the Inner Mongol Nationalists, was absent, but I saw a secretary, who was very obliging in offering to help in any way he could and seemed suitably impressed by my imposing-looking Chinese passport. This was the first and the last I saw of the Autonomous Government of Inner Mongolia. Whether they still exist, suspended between the Chinese provinces of Northern China, Russian Mongolia and Japanese Manchuria, I do not know.

* * *

The next morning, while we were breakfasting in Gonzell's yurts at 6 a.m., the news was brought us that the convoy of Sin-sui trucks were in sight. They came pouring over the hill from the west, past the monastery and across the stream to the Chinese bazaar at irregular intervals. George Soderbom dashed off in his two-seater Ford and brought his brother back in triumph soon after eight. Seldom have I seen anyone look more pleased than Gustav Soderbom on his arrival at Pai-ling Miao after being lost to the world for over three years. Unshaven, unwashed and unkempt, dressed in an ancient pair of trousers, skin jacket and Tartar cap, he stood there beaming with joy and receiving our congratulations and those of his Mongol and Chinese friends. The Sin-sui trucks, returning empty, had made a record journey from Hami to Pai-ling Miao in ten days, starting daily at 2 a.m. in the dark and driving through to late at night ; a feat of real endurance on the part of drivers, passengers and crews, urged on by the

[1] This is the usual romanization of the Chinese character pronounced *Dö*.

Mr. Gonzell in Front of his Mongolian Home at Pai-ling Miao

...rge (the taller) and Gustav Soderbom, at Pai-ling Miao, September 20, 1935

Breaking Camp at Pai-ling Miao, Early Morning, September 20

Wa Sha-tzu!

prospect of the fleshpots of China after the risks and hardships of the desert trail.

*   *   *

After the Soderbom reunion the brothers left for Suiyuan, while we turned our trucks up the trail to the west. In spite of a late start our day's run was a good one, to a camp on the banks of a marshy stream over a hundred miles from Pai-ling Miao. For the first fifty miles the going was very good, across vast undulating steppes of grass, crossing ridge after ridge and passing from one flat valley bottom to another. These prairies are treeless and empty, save for the antelope and occasional flocks and herds of sheep, cattle, ponies and camels. The antelope were constantly in view, galloping along parallel to our course and then following one another across the front of the trucks. We met them all the way to Kashgar, but never in such quantities as on the first few days.

Fifty miles out we passed through a stretch of sandy country, with Chinese farms, called the Yang Ch'ang-tzu Kou (" Sheep Gut Valley " or " The Valley of Sheep Ranches," according to the Chinese characters used to write the name). Here we stuck several times, but extricated ourselves easily enough with a little spade-work. From now on the cry of *Wa Sha-tzu* (" Dig out from Sand ") became all too familiar for the rest of the journey. The truck would come to a slow stop in the sand, a fruitless attempt would be made to get out on low gear ; and then *Wa Sha-tzu !* and all hands to the spades.

On the next day's run the sand grew worse and warned us that we were approaching the Gobi. Near Ho-sa-tu, a Chinese tax station and small military post at the junction of trails running east and

west and north and south, we met the only motor
vehicles that we saw all the way to Hami. One
was a Mongolian Government truck from Pai-ling
Miao ; the other flew the Japanese flag. Whence
had it come and whither was it bound ? No doubt
its occupants entered our trucks and union jacks
in their notebooks with a similar query.

Beyond Ho-sa-tu the camel trail passes through
the Lao-hu Shan (" Tiger Mountains ") by a narrow
pass and the motor route swings to the north-west.
Crossing the brow of a hill, we reached Uni-ussu
(" Cow Water "), a desolate little camp of yurts on
the banks of a stream flowing north. This was
another Chinese tax station and military post, the
last on the road to the west. The tax official and the
garrison of two soldiers seemed oppressed by the vast
solitude of the place. We camped at Uni-ussu and
spent the afternoon purchasing, slaughtering and cutting up a sheep. I went for a walk, but there was
nothing to see beyond the camels picturesquely sil-
houetted against the background of desert and sky.
The tax official, a stout Chinese Moslem from Pao-
t'ou, seemed surly and disinterested, perhaps owing
to his disappointment at finding that we were untax-
able material.

* * *

Uni-ussu marks the beginning of the desert and
of more difficult country for motor traffic ; and it
was from somewhere in this neighbourhood that
Serat and Gustav Soderbom on their first through
trip to Hami made their adventurous dash through
Outer Mongolia to the Etsin Gol. The motor trail
now turns south and then west, rejoining the camel
trail after its exit from the Lao-hu K'ou (" Tiger

Pass "). Fifteen miles out we reached the edge of a plateau with a wonderful view over an immensity of desert stretching westwards to the horizon far below. We descended through a desolation of sand, whins, tussocks, gravel and rock, like some super-bunker of a golfer's nightmare ; and from then on we were lost in the profundities of the Gobi desert, extending, save for the oasis of the Etsin Gol, for a thousand miles to Hami.

We were following a camel trail and the tracks of the Sin-sui trucks and we passed several wells with the yurts of Chinese *Mai-mai Jen*. These enterprising traders, mostly the agents of Chinese firms in Pao-t'ou and Suiyuan, are established all along the closed frontier of Outer Mongolia, collecting Mongolian produce in exchange for brick tea and Chinese goods. We met and conversed with a Mohammedan camel caravan carrying brick tea to Hami, twelve days out from Suiyuan ; they expected to be another two months on the road ; then another Chinese caravan two weeks out from Pao-t'ou and bound for Kansu by the desert road ; and some Mongol lamas returning from an alms-collecting expedition to Kumbum monastery near the Kokonor. Such is the life of the Gobi camel trails. But this early part of the route was relatively populous ; and later on we were to travel for hundreds of miles through the empty Gobi without meeting a soul on the road.

The going was bad on this day's run and we suffered many minor stoppages in sand, usually when crossing the dry, sandy beds of dead streams. We were also cursed by a following wind, which, with so much low gear work, meant boiling radiators and frequent stops to replenish them with water.

We were now somewhere near, but thirty to forty

miles to the north of, a big monastery called Shantan Miao, on the main camel trail, " The Winding Road " followed by Mr. Lattimore, through the middle of the Inner Mongolian Gobi.[1]   The " Winding Road " branching off to the south-west, is impassable to motor traffic and the new motor trail edges its way by minor camel trails, dry river-beds and desert detours through the sands along the Outer Mongolian border farther north.

* * *

Seventy miles from Uni-ussu we reached a place called Bayen Unter, a few yurts under a hill which is a landmark from afar.   Beyond are impassable sandhills, barring the way to the west.   Here we left the trail we had been following and plunged left-handed over trackless desert hills, up and down which our trucks climbed like mechanized yaks.   We had done nothing quite so alarming before, but Serat assured me he knew where he was going.   And so it proved. For we soon reached and turned westwards along the dry bed of a dead river called the Meringen Gol, which had been discovered by Serat and Gustav Soderbom when, on the return trip from their first journey to Hami, they found this route through the impassable sands.   The bed of the Meringen Gol was trackless but furnished good going and we careered down it at twenty miles per hour, which seemed a tremendous and dashing speed in a three-ton truck on hard desert when one does not know what lies ahead.   On our right were the big sandhills, with their tops smoking in the wind.   After ten miles or so we left the Meringen Gol and climbed out right-handed onto a gravel plateau, where we rejoined the

[1] See *The Desert Road to Turkistan*, by Owen Lattimore.

At Uni-Ussu, on the Edge of the Gobi

Heavy Going in the Gobi, near Hoyer Amatu, September 24

Midday Halt, in the Gobi, beyond Bandin Tologoi

Camp in the Gobi, Well of Kuku Tologoi

Meeting with the First Torgut Mongol from the Etsin Gol

The First Torgut Mongol from the Etsin Gol

Refugee Mongols from Outer Mongolia Encamped at Wayen Torrai, East Etsin

Chinese Wireless Station at Wayen Torrai, East Etsin Gol, October 4

trail we had left before Bayen Unter. On the northern horizon lay another line of enormous sand-hills, *Ta Sha-mo*, as Serat called them, stretching along the Outer Mongolian border.[1] Here we had a long hunt for the well at which we were to camp. Serat knew roughly where it was, but it took us nearly an hour to find it. Without a guide who knows the road, it would be impossible to find many of these wells, which, unless marked as they sometimes are by a settlement of yurts, are often invisible a hundred yards away. Serat knew them all, and which were sweet, which bitter and which indifferent. This was a good one of clean sweet water, its sides neatly lined with dead desert wood, and its cover in good repair.

* * *

The weather had been warm and obviously on the break for some days, and on September 23 we awoke to find steady rain which continued all day. Rain was the last kind of trouble I had expected in the Gobi, but for the next few days wet weather was to cause us much misfortune and delay. We remained all that day in camp, moving carefully about in the tiny tents to avoid touching the sodden cotton cloth and felt, which were moderately watertight as long as there was no contact with the things inside. The next morning it was still raining, but soon cleared up. Serat had misgivings about the state of the desert, but we decided to make a start.

We travelled north of west across a gravel plateau, which, I was told, was normally good going. But the surface of the whole desert had been so soaked and softened by the rain that we soon began sticking,

[1] *Sha-mo*, a Chinese word, means "sandy desert." *Gobi* means "gravel desert."

first one truck and then the other, sometimes axle-deep, in the soft sandy mud. It was a case of dig and dig again, with frequent recourse to the rope mats; and a desperately disheartening job at that; for it was certain, when one truck had at last been extricated and got going again, that it or the other one would stick again a little farther on. The twin peaks of Hoyer Amatu, marking the neighbourhood of our immediate destination, were in sight all the time, but it seemed as though we should never get any nearer to them. Antelope ran across our front and stopped to look at the bogged trucks in the queer way they have.

It took us most of the day to cover twenty miles, and then we reached the first of a number of sandy streamlets and our troubles became worse again. Finally we crossed some higher rocky ground to descend to the last stream, down the normally dry bed of which, Serat said, lay our road to Hoyer Amatu. The surrounding country, rocks and sandhills, looked quite impassable and there seemed to be no alternative but to follow down the stream. We tried to take it at speed, the only way of getting through soft ground; and almost at once the new truck, leading, stuck hopelessly, up to both back axles, in soft sandy mud. Overtaken by darkness we had to camp in the sandhills near by. As the truck threatened to sink ever deeper in its sandy bog, we had to work through the night, unloading, digging under the wheels, jacking them up, and inserting planks and rope mats underneath. It was nearly midnight before we had the truck out and parked on dry sand and were able to retire exhausted to food and rest.

This was one of several occasions (the others were

to follow) when I wondered whether we should get through ; and, pondering over our unhappy situation, I thought what an easy prey we should be for wandering bands of brigands or patrols from across the frontier line.

* * *

After a cold night the day broke to a perfect morning, hot sun and still blue skies. After drying out our things and resting in the sun, we started off again at midday to find our way somehow or other through the wilderness of sand and rocks. We plunged along, up and down rocks and sandhills, making successful, but very slow, progress, as we had to have two men walking ahead to pick out the route. At length we began to descend and rejoined the trail which we had had to leave the previous day owing to the soft ground. Our immediate troubles were now at an end and a good road soon brought us to Hoyer Amatu, a well and few yurts in the middle of a vast desert plain, bounded on the north by the hills of the Outer Mongolian frontier, here only ten to fifteen miles off.

We had arranged to pick up our first petrol dump at Hoyer Amatu. It was there all right. But we were disappointed to learn that the camels carrying the remainder had only just passed through and could not be expected to reach the last depot, on the farther side of the Etsin Gol, for another two to three weeks. We had therefore only too much time to spare ; and we rested another day at Hoyer Amatu to allow the desert ahead more time to dry out after the rain, while we killed a sheep, greased the trucks and had a general wash and brush up.

* * *

Friday, September 27, was another black day in the expedition's diary. We made an early start and fared well at first, finding good going across the desert plain. Beyond Abter well we struck a bad patch, where the desert surface was soft gravel, through which we kept breaking and sticking time after time. Then Serat left the trail, and we struck off north-wards across the trackless desert in search of firmer ground. I was uneasy whenever this occurred, for there was comfort in following the camel trails and still more in the sight of the Sin-sui wheel tracks. For a time we made better progress, and then disaster overtook us. The old truck started an ominous " knock " somewhere in its transmission, got rapidly worse, and was finally brought to a standstill in a state, as was only too evident, of complete collapse.

There was nothing for it but to camp where we were and take the truck down and ascertain the damage. It was midday and grilling hot and our water supply was limited to what we carried with us for emergency use. Fortunately fuel was, as usual in the Gobi, available, in the form of dead tamarisk bushes and other brushwood.

This was another occasion when I wondered whether we should ever get to Sinkiang, and when the superiority of motor transport over the camel caravan seemed at least an open question. The Gobi can be terrible and awe-inspiring, whether in the glittering heat of noon or the icy cold of night, espe-cially when one is marooned in its desolation, without water, and with a motor truck in process of being taken to pieces. The spot where we were camped was a typical bit of Gobi country, barren and desolate, lifeless save for antelope and lizard, and the ground strewn with coloured pebbles, white, yellow, red, green and blue, many resembling prehistoric artifacts. The place was marked on my map as " Breakdown Camp " and I never want to see it again.

Turning up my diary of this anxious day, I see that by 4.30 p.m. we had got the wheels off and the back axle out of the truck, removed it bodily, opened it up and discovered the damage ; the differential driving gear, than which there is no more vital part in the truck's transmission, was completely smashed. At some point or other in the tremendous straining of the last stoppage in the sand the teeth of the driving gear had given way. Fortunately we had a new part in our liberal supply of spares. When we ceased work owing to darkness at 7 p.m. the new driving gear had been fitted ; and by noon the next day we had the back axle in place again and were ready for the road. We had been held up for twenty-four hours on the job, which would have been a big enough one in a well-equipped garage. Serat, Chomcha and Kuo had done it in the middle of the desert.

Our practice was for the new truck, driven by me and Serat, to lead the way, followed by the old one driven by Chomcha and Kuo. Whenever the latter was no longer in sight one of the men seated on the load behind us would knock on the back of our cab to apprise us that something was wrong. These knocks were frequent, usually presaging nothing more serious than a stoppage in the sand ; but after our experiences that day, I never heard one without a sinking feeling in the diaphragm and a surge of anxiety as to what was going to happen next.

*　　*　　*

We soon regained the Sin-sui trail, but our troubles were not yet at an end. We had hoped to reach the well at Yingen, which Serat believed to be not far off, for the night, for we were now reduced to our last five-gallon drum of water. But the Sin-sui wheel tracks here wandered off in the wrong direction, heading north-west for the mountains and the Outer Mongolian border ; while, with heavy going, much low gear work and a following wind, the radiators boiled and had frequently to be replenished from our diminishing water supply. We decided temporarily to abandon one truck, transfer all the water to the other, and leave the trail to strike across the desert in the direction where Serat believed the Yingen well to lie. But just at this moment we came on the unexpected but welcome sight of three Chinese digging a well ; and, what was better still, they had just reached water ; it was only a muddy yellow sump at the bottom of the pit, but enough to fill a bucket every half-hour or so. Our immediate anxieties were now at an end and we camped near the embryo well assured of a safe if restricted supply of water. The Chinese and Mongols connected with the motor transport trade of the Gobi can tell some grim stories about motor-truck travel and water shortage in the desert.

The three Chinese well-diggers turned out to be Sin-sui Company employees, marooned here with a broken-down truck and awaiting the next convoy with the necessary spare parts. The puzzle of our whereabouts was later cleared up. In the file of information concerning the route which I had collected was a note about the well at Yingen, which, I was warned, lay actually on the Outer Mongolian border ; so that one had to be careful to camp south of a certain sandhill in order to be sure of remaining on the right side of the frontier. But there are bad sands round Yingen well, which, the Sin-sui men told us, could not now be reached by motors at all ; and the Sin-sui trucks had worked out a new detour to the north, cutting for a few miles through Outer Mongolian territory. That was where we were now camped, five to ten miles north of Yingen well, in Outer Mongolia. The Outer Mongol patrols remain, however, on the other side of a low mountain range and do not interfere with the motor trail. The Hardt-Citroen party, Serat told me, had also lost their bearings in this neighbourhood, trying to get round the Yingen sands, and had run up against the forbidden frontiers of Outer Mongolia.

I was not at all happy at finding ourselves camped beyond the frontier ; and to make matters worse, black clouds coming up from the south-east turned during the night into another downpour ; so that we were detained in this camp for another two days. This was, however, the last rain we were to encounter on the whole journey.

In the evening a Mongol rode up on a camel with a sheep to sell to the Sin-sui Chinese. He turned out to be the local inhabitant, established with his yurts, family and flocks and herds on the banks of some lagoons a few miles off. He confirmed that we were in Outer Mongolia, but did not appear to find anything out of order in our presence there, and was only too pleased to sell us another sheep. The next day I walked over with my gun to the lagoons, tucked away behind enormous sandhills two to three miles north-north-west of our camp ; an incredibly remote spot, never visited, I suppose, by a European before. There were plenty of wildfowl about, and I returned with two mallard.

Talking later on with our new friends, the Sin-sui

Chinese, they told us how they were engaged on a three-year contract and of their life and work in the desert. They were supplied with two rifles for self-defence, and were able to vary their menu of flour and mutton with an occasional antelope ; but they were chary, they said, of firing shots on the Outer Mongolian border. I decided *not* to go duck-shooting again to the lagoons !

*   *   *

We took the road again on October 1 and, turning south, soon had the satisfaction of knowing that we were back on the right side of the frontier. Before going far we met two Mongols, a man and his wife, on camels, heading south. They were refugees from Outer Mongolia, fleeing from the communist paradise there. We met more of these refugees later on. The going was still bad, with much heavy sand, and we were seldom out of low gear ; so that we did not do badly with a day's run of fifty miles. We camped at a place called Bandin Tologoi, consisting of half a dozen yurts, two mud huts, and several caravan tents, near a good well of sweet water tucked away amongst the sandhills. Bandin Tologoi seemed quite a Gobi metropolis. There was a Sin-sui Company depot, a Chinese trader or two, and a tax station of sorts. The place appeared to owe its existence to its situation at the junction of our route with a trail from Ninghsia and the Alashan country to Urga and Outer Mongolia. This was one of the principal lines of communication in 1926–7 between Feng Yü-hsiang's *Kuo-min-chün* forces and the U.S.S.R. ; and it was probably by this route that Borodin and Percy Ch'en escaped from China by motor across the Gobi

56

desert in the summer of 1927.[1] To the south of Bandin Tologoi lies the sandy depression of the Goitso, which is one of the obstacles to east and west motor traffic by the main camel trail, Mr. Lattimore's "Winding Road."

Soon after leaving Bandin Tologoi we struck another bad patch, soft clay below a gravel surface. One of the trucks became embedded, with its chassis frame and back axle reposing on the ground. It looked impossible to get it out. But we did so, after two hours' toil, unloading, digging out the rear wheels, jacking them up, inserting planks underneath, and laying rope mats in front. This proved, however, our last serious stoppage for some days, as we now worked up on to higher ground with better going through low ranges of sandy, rocky hills. Here and there between the ranges were plains of hard flat gravel across which we hummed in fine style at twenty-five and even thirty miles per hour. As we advanced the Gobi became increasingly grim and barren, even the sparse tamarisk bushes and camel scrub giving out ; a scene of hideous desolation, overwhelming in its immensity and emptiness, yet with an awe-inspiring beauty of its own ; ravines and hills grotesquely shaped, valleys and slopes of dusty gravel, many mirages, and here and there an antelope; no other sign of life. Each camp was like the last, our three tents pitched, facing south-east (to shelter

---

[1] Borodin was the Russian adviser who inspired the South China revolution of 1926. When the Chinese later on turned against the Russians and the communists, Borodin fled from Hankow accompanied by Percy Ch'en, the son of Eugene Ch'en, the Foreign Minister of the Revolutionary Government. The story of their flight across Mongolia is told in *China's Millions*, by Anna Louise Strong.

from the prevailing winds), near the solitary well surrounded by bare gravel desert and queer misshapen hills.

We passed our petrol camels, five-and-twenty exhausted looking animals, lightly loaded, for camels, with six five-gallon drums of petrol apiece. The camp of the three cameleers, Chinese from Suiyuan, lacking all the small luxuries that make camp life endurable, looked the acme of discomfort; but Chinese standards of comfort are not ours and they seemed happy enough seated in their tattered Mongol tent and sipping bowls of evil-looking tea. For days on end we met no other travellers.

* * *

On the third day from Bandin Tologoi we entered a region of coloured hills of sandstone, blue, green, yellow, brown and red. Suddenly we came upon a solitary figure, and as we drew nearer we descried a Mongol mounted on a camel and carrying a native prong gun slung across his back. We stopped and conversed and found him to be an antelope-hunter from the Etsin Gol, the first Torgut Mongol we had met. With his pigtail and old-fashioned Manchu hat and well-conditioned camel, he made a picturesque figure, perfectly appropriate to the background of barren desert. For us he was a harbinger of our approach to the promised land of the Etsin Gol and the end of the first lap of the desert journey.

Soon after from the top of the last range of hills we saw a black smudge on the horizon which resolved itself into a line of trees marking the western edge of the oasis of the Etsin Gol. Descending across a sandy plain, we reached the poplars, a glorious sight in their autumn foliage of greens and yellows, bronze and gold. We pitched our camp for the first time under trees, and on thin grass, instead of gravel desert. Near by were some caravan tents and a few yurts, backed by enormous sandhills covered with tamarisks. The place is called Wayen Torrai and marks the point where the Gobi motor trail meets the oasis of the Etsin Gol. One of the yurts was a Sin-sui Company depot and another housed the newly established Chinese Government Wireless Station. We were therefore in this remote spot once again in touch with the outer world and I was able to report my arrival to my wife, to the Embassy in China, and to the Chinese authorities in Turkistan.

CHAPTER IV

INTERLUDE ON THE ETSIN GOL

The Etsin Gol oasis—Wayen Torrai and Karakoto—
Journey round the twin lakes—Ulanchonchi on the
West Etsin Gol—Life during our stay on the Etsin Gol—
Mongolian camel trails to Sinkiang—Conditions in
Outer Mongolia—The Torgut Mongols of the Etsin
Gol—Arrival of our petrol caravan.

THE Etsin Gol rises in the mountains of the Kokonor
border and waters the oases of Western Kansu before
flowing north into the desert. Beyond the township
of Maomu, on the edge of Kansu, it splits up into
two or three main and other subsidiary channels and
flows north for some 200 miles through the Gobi to
end in the twin salt lakes of Gashun Nor and Sogo
Nor, at the back of beyond, on the Outer Mongolian
border. This is the Etsin Gol oasis, about 200 miles
long by thirty to fifty broad, a country of desert
poplars, tamarisks, and sparse, reedy grass, inhabited
by a tribe of Torgut Mongols. Though it is a semi-
desert area, it seems to the weary Gobi traveller a
haven of greenery, water and repose. Stein and
Sven Hedin have explored its rivers and twin lakes,
motor trucks have ploughed its sands, and even
aeroplanes have paid the place a visit ; for it was
here that the machines of the Eurasia Company
landed and took off on one of their courageous
flights to Sinkiang some years ago. Wayen Torrai
and the Etsin Gol can therefore no longer claim the
attractions of the unknown. Yet the only published
map I could lay hands on that was of any use for
our journey was a crude Chinese chart of the Sin-sui

Company's motor trail. The best existing British maps were completely blank for most of the way along the route we followed from Suiyuan to the borders of Chinese Turkistan.

Wayen Torrai, the place where we were camped, lies on the edge of the oasis, to the east of the eastern-most branch of the Etsin Gol. Somewhere in the big sandhills to the south is hidden the dead, sand-buried city of Karakoto, called Etsina by Marco Polo, in whose day it was a flourishing city of the ancient Tangut Kingdom. The Mongol name *Karakoto* and the Chinese name *Hei Ch'eng* both mean " The Black City." The Chinese also give the name " Black River " (*Hei Ho*) to the upper reaches of the Etsin Gol in Kansu. The ruins of Karakoto have been visited by several explorers, including Sir Aurel Stein, who identifies it with Marco Polo's Etsina.

* * *

One of the questions often debated since the start of our expedition was how we were to cross the rivers of the Etsin Gol. In the summer the waters of the main river are mostly used up by the farmers of Kansu on the upper reaches for irrigation purposes and the streams of the Etsin Gol are dry ; in the winter they are frozen ; and in both these conditions it is possible, if one knows the way through the sand-hills, to drive motor trucks across the various channels of the river. In the autumn months, however, the main branches of the Etsin Gol contain too much water to be crossed and motor traffic has to make the long detour round the salt lakes to the north, involving a hard journey of over 150 miles through a terribly desolate part of the Gobi, with a corresponding adjustment of estimates of petrol consumption for the whole route.

From the inquiries we made at Wayen Torrai it was certain that there was too much water in the main streams to make the direct journey across the oasis ; and on October 5 we started on the detour round the lakes. There are no wells on the way and we had to carry our own water supply, consisting of twelve five-gallon drums, enough for the trucks and ourselves for three days. It proved a hard and wearisome journey, across a vast desert plain of sand and gravel, dotted with dead tamarisk bushes. We passed close to the smaller lake, Sogo Nor, crossing a salt-encrusted depression on its shores ; but, with the shimmering mirages everywhere, it was difficult to distinguish the real water from the sham. The desert was gravel over sand, and, though we did not stick often, we were grinding along in low gear most of the way. We camped the first night, after covering seventy miles, in low hills to the north of Gashun Nor. The day's journey left on my mind an impression of ploughing endlessly through the gravelly sand on first and second gears, bumping over tamarisk ground, boiling radiator water, and shimmering, desolate, salt-encrusted desert. Along the northern horizon ran a range of mountains, which, Serat said, lay in Outer Mongolia. We met no living thing, not even an antelope, and seemed infinitely remote from anywhere.

The next day we crossed the top of the range, with fine views over Gashun Nor to the south and the hills and mountains of Outer Mongolia to the north. We seemed to be quite close to the Noyen Bogdo range, which by the map lies well inside Outer Mongolia, and we must have been very near, if not across, the frontier line. Then we struck a big camel trail, running north and south, from Urga and Outer

Mongolia to Suchou and Kansu. The camel tracks, beaten down by the footprints of generations of camels, afford a better surface for motor traffic than the rest of the desert, and we found the going excellent as soon as we turned south along this trail. Indeed, for some miles where we crossed a dry lake bottom, which had evidently once formed part of Gashun Nor, we sped along at thirty miles per hour over a surface as firm and flat as that of an arterial road at home.

In the late afternoon we reached sand and trees again, passing a ruined fort of great antiquity. Then we came to a prominent tower, built up out of dead tamarisk wood, which marked the junction of the north to south Urga–Suchou road with the east to west China–Sinkiang camel trail ; and arrived soon after at our destination, a remote little tax station called Ulan-chonchi, consisting of a yurt and a mud hut, on the west bank of the westernmost branch of the Etsin Gol. We were well pleased at having covered in two days and without incident the 165 miles of desert round the lakes from Wayen Torrai.

* * *

The residents of Ulan-chonchi comprised the tax official, a Chinese from Peking, and his staff of a half a dozen Mongols and Chinese. The duties of the latter were to ride out into the desert and spy for passing caravans and ensure they did not escape the tax collector's net. So simple a system illustrates the law-abiding character of the Chinese and Mongol cameleers. We were told that the tax station, formerly under Kansu, was now under the Mongol Government at Pai-ling Miao. But these fiscal arrangements in China's borderlands are apt to be vague and ephemeral.

Behind the tax collector's hut was a derelict motor truck, lying in the sand and stripped of everything removable. They said it was a broken-down memento of a tour of inspection paid to these parts by General Ho Ying-ch'in, Chinese Minister for War. By a particular irony it was stamped " Reo Speed Truck," a product of the U.S.A. ; buried lopsidedly in the sand, it would never speed again.

We pitched our tents, as usual facing south-east, overlooking the nearly dry bed of the westernmost branch of the Etsin Gol. Behind us a flat expanse of desert stretched to the western horizon. In front, on the farther side of the stream-bed, were sandhills, tamarisk bushes and poplars, golden in their autumn foliage. A mile or two beyond the sandhills to the east was one of the main branches of the river with a considerable flow of water. We made our camp as comfortable as we could, for we knew that we should have to wait there for a week or ten days for our petrol camels to arrive. Ulan-chonchi would be one of the last places one would choose for a prolonged stay ; but we were glad of the rest. I occupied myself with strolls round the neighbourhood, shooting, reading and writing, and the days slipped easily by. The weather was typical of the Gobi autumn, frost at night, grilling hot sun at midday, and every afternoon a strong wind from the west. I used to rise when the sun had begun to warm the air and breakfast about 8 a.m. off tea, fresh milk, and home-made bread baked in our camp oven ; spend the morning with my papers, books and maps ; lunch off coffee, sheep's liver or kidney and bacon, bread, butter and honey, a delicious meal ; a stroll with the gun in the afternoon ; and dinner about 7 p.m., soup, local mutton or game, vegetables and stewed

Desolation of the Gobi, near Sogo Nor

Camp North of Gashun Nor, on the Outer Mongolian Border, October 5

The Tax Station at Ulanchonchi, West Etsin Gol

Camp at Ulanchonchi; The Kitchen Tent

The *Tograk* or *Wu-t'ung Shu*, Poplar and Willow Growing Out of one Trunk, West Etsin Gol

a *Tsao'rh Shu* (" Sand Date Tree "), Oleaster or Wild Olive, West Etsin Gol

Torgut Mongols at Ulanchonchi, West Etsin Gol

Torgut Mongol at Ulanchonchi ; in the Background Loading Petrol on to the Trucks

dried fruits. It was life reduced to its simplest terms. No morning paper, no evening wireless news. Though actually we might have had the latter ; for our trucks were parked outside the tents and George Soderbom, in his capacity as agent for Mr. Henry Ford, had done his best to sell me a Ford car wireless receiving set. I had refused this luxury because when I tried it out at Suiyuan we could get little but unintelligible sounds of music and propaganda from Nanking and Habarovsk mingled with the unearthly cracklings of Gobi atmospherics, and because I thought that any wireless set would probably provoke in Turkistan suspicions that I was secretly colloguing with Delhi or Nanking.

There were some quite attractive spots round our camp at Ulan-chonchi, one might almost call them forest glades, under the big poplars. But I soon learned that it was dangerous to wander far from camp without taking a compass and bearings of one's path. The poplar trees (in Chinese *Wu-t'ung Shu*, in Turki *Tograk*) were peculiar in that they often comprised a poplar and a willow growing out of one trunk. There were also big berry-bearing trees of the oleaster type (in Chinese *Sha Tsao'rh Shu*—" Sand Date Tree ") and two varieties of tamarisk (*Hung-liu* and *San-ch'uan-liu*). I had hoped to find pheasants, but saw none. We shot several mallard along the river, occasional sandgrouse and a bustard. But the shooting on the whole was disappointing.

We made friends with the tax official and his minions and passed the time of day with the merchants and cameleers of the rare caravans that wandered through. All were interested and pleased to meet such distinguished visitors from far-away Peking ; for to the Mongols and camel-pullers of these north-

5

western marches the old capital of the Chinese Empire is still the first city of the world. Most of the travellers we met were bound to or from Suchou in Western Kansu. Some were Khalkha Mongols, refugees from Outer Mongolia, and it was at Ulan-chonchi that I first saw the Outer Mongol silver coins, well-minted pieces, about the size of the old silver rouble, inscribed with Mongol characters and bearing the national emblem of Mongolia, a sun, surmounted by a flame above a recumbent crescent moon [1] ; the inscriptions (as translated to me by Serat into Chinese) read : *One tugrik. For use throughout Mongolia. Fine silver eighteen grammes.*

* * *

On this first lap of our journey from Suiyuan to the Etsin Gol we had travelled for hundreds of miles along and often in sight of the Outer Mongolian border. Roughly speaking, Outer Mongolia lies to the north, and Inner Mongolia to the south, of the Gobi desert.[2] Our route to the Etsin Gol had taken

[1] According to Geleta (*The New Mongolia*), this device was the crest of Genghis Khan.

[2] Under the Chinese Empire Mongolia was divided into Outer and Inner, north and south of the Gobi respectively. Both were ruled, under Chinese, or rather Manchu, suzerainty, by the native Mongol princes, but Inner Mongolia was naturally in closer touch with China. The representatives of the Emperor of China in Outer Mongolia were the Manchu Ambans at Urga, Kobdo and Uliasutai. Outer Mongolia has now broken away from China ; while Inner Mongolia is divided up into the three Chinese provinces of Chahar, Suiyuan and Ninghsia. The Inner Mongols have a standing grievance against China in that Chinese settlers have for generations been invading and plough-ing up the Mongolian grasslands. And the Japanese, working in from Manchuria, are trying hard to bring Inner Mongolia

us through the northern part of the Gobi and for much of the way the horizon on our right hand had been bounded by the mountains marking the frontier. Beyond these mountains lay the grasslands of Outer Mongolia affording by all accounts much easier ground for motor traffic. In former days the main camel caravan trail to Sinkiang ran through Outer Mongolia. This was the route followed by early European travellers, including General Younghusband in the eighties of last century ; and, were it still available, it would probably afford the best and easiest route for motor traffic between China and Turkistan. When, after the Great War, the frontiers of Outer Mongolia were closed, the China–Sinkiang caravan trade had to find another route and the trail through the Inner Mongolian Gobi *via* Shan-tan Miao (Mr. Lattimore's " Winding Road ") came in this way into use. This camel trail, " The Winding Road," passes through the centre of the Gobi and is, owing to the sands beyond Shan-tan Miao, impassable for motor traffic. The present motor trail along the Outer Mongolian border was then discovered by Serat, the Soderboms and other pioneers. As we struggled through its sands we looked longingly at the mountains to the north and the forbidden land beyond, where, we were told, lay good firm camel trails and grassy steppes. Often, gazing from truck or camp at the line of hills on the horizon, I wondered what was really going on beyond the forbidden frontier line.

It is indeed difficult to arrive at any definite conclusions in regard to conditions in Outer Mongolia.

under their influence. It was to conciliate the Inner Mongols that the Chinese Government recently established " The Autonomous Government of Inner Mongolia " which we met at Pai-ling Miao.

Little or no reliable information on the subject is obtainable in China or Inner Mongolia ; and such information as one may gather will probably be propaganda or opinion highly coloured by prejudice for or against the Bolshevik régime. Outer Mongolia was formerly a dependency of the old Chinese, or rather Manchu, Empire. After the Chinese Revolution of 1911 the Mongols broke away from the new Chinese Republic and established an independent Government of Outer Mongolia, recognizing the nominal suzerainty of China, but under Russian influence. Up to this point developments in Mongolia had (with the substitution of Russia for Great Britain) run parallel to those in Tibet. After the Great War and the Russian Revolution the Chinese Government in 1919 and 1920 sought to reassert themselves in Outer Mongolia, tore up the treaties made with the Russians and the Mongols, and sent a military expedition to Urga. I visited Urga at this time and witnessed the reoccupation of Outer Mongolia by the Chinese. But the Chinese effort was short-lived. A force of White Russians, led by a strange and horrible figure, the Baron Ungern-Sternburg, descended on Urga, chased out the Chinese troops, massacred Chinese and Jews, and established a reign of terror. The White occupation of Urga afforded a pretext for intervention to the Bolsheviks, who in turn descended on Outer Mongolia, drove out the mad Baron and his Whites, deprived the Mongol princes and lamas of their power and established a communist Mongol Republic. This astonishing transition from the old Mongolia to the new was hastened by the death in 1924 of the Bogdo Hutuktu, the Urga Reincarnation, a lama pontiff ranking in importance only after the Dalai and Panshen Lamas of Tibet.

Little is known in China and the West of what has happened since in Outer Mongolia, except that the Mongol People's Republic and the Soviet Government in Urga appear to be firmly established. The Russians naturally lay themselves open to the charge of having raped Mongolia just as the Japanese have raped Manchuria ; and the Soviet Ambassador at Nanking must have had many embarrassing discussions on the subject with the *Wai Chiao Pu*.[1] But the Russians have been clever, and probably to a large extent successful, in Outer Mongolia, and have enjoyed the great advantage of being able to work through Russian Buriats (who are Siberian Mongols) ; and it would be rash to assume that the Outer Mongols wish to return to the Chinese or any other fold. It may be that, as in the former Khanates of Russian Central Asia, while many of the older Mongols are restive and dissatisfied under red rule, the younger generation are being formed under Russian tutelage into something so different as to make it impossible usefully to compare the new Mongolia with the old. The Lama Church, the Buddhism of Mongolia and Tibet, has picturesque features and beauties of its own. But there can hardly be any question of its stifling and deadening effect on the life of the common people. In the new Mongolia the temporal power of the lamas has been broken, and holy Urga has electric light, motor-buses and aeroplanes, cinemas and modern schools and hospitals.[2]

Whatever the truth about its real condition may be,

[1] The Chinese Foreign Office.
[2] Urga, formerly known to the Mongols as Bogdo Kuren (" The Holy Monastery ") and to the Chinese as Ta-kuren or Ta-kulun, has now been renamed Ulan Batur Koto (" The City of Red Heroes ").

Outer Mongolia under red rule is a land that guards its secrets well. The old trade and intercourse with China are at an end and the frontiers with Inner Mongolia and Manchuria are strictly closed. The Russians will tell one that the Mongol People's Republic is not a constituent part of the U.S.S.R., but a State organized on a similar basis. But permission to enter Outer Mongolia can only be obtained from Moscow; Moscow will probably refer the applicant to Urga, and Urga has no official relations with any country other than the Russian Soviet. The result, from the point of view of the rest of the world, is to cut the Outer Mongols off from all foreign intercourse other than with the U.S.S.R.

* * *

The Mongols of the Etsin Gol oasis belong ethnologically neither to Outer nor Inner Mongolia, but to the tribe of Western Mongols called *Torguts*,[1] who inhabit the mountain uplands of Chinese Turkistan. There were local Torgut Mongols in the neighbourhood of our camp, pasturing their flocks of sheep and herds of camels on the thin reedy grass. They were mostly poor-looking specimens and rode about on donkeys, which are inappropriate mounts for members of the proud and horsey Mongol race. One evening I received a visit from a Mongol official, an old man of seventy, who made a stately approach out of the tamarisk scrub on a fine camel led by a retainer on a white pony. We drank tea and conversed about nothing in particular. He brought me greetings from the Torgut Mongol Prince of Etsin Gol, whose residence was somewhere in the interior of the oasis

[1] See page 129.

but who was absent on a pilgrimage to Kumbum monastery in the Kokonor.

*　　*　　*

The days passed, the sun shone, the west wind blew, and we began to grow anxious at the non-arrival of our petrol caravan.　On October 16 I was out shooting duck and sandgrouse when a procession of tired-looking camels filed slowly out of the tamarisk scrub.　Our petrol had arrived at last.　For the rest of the day all hands were busy loading the trucks and preparing for a fresh start the next morning.　As we did not know what sort of a reception to expect in Sinkiang and whether or not Russian stocks of petrol would be available for us there, we had to work out our supplies to last through to Kashgar ; and, Ulan-chonchi being our last petrol dump, we had to carry the entire stock with us from this point.　I see from my diary that when we left Ulan-chonchi the new truck was loaded with 108 five-gallon drums of petrol, weighing 4,000 odd pounds, *plus* many other items of baggage and equipment and three or four men, probably not far short of four tons in all.

CHAPTER V

THE BLACK GOBI : FROM THE ETSIN GOL TO HAMI

WE left Ulan-chonchi and the Etsin Gol on October 17. The next lap, 400 miles to Hami, lay across the Black Gobi, an empty no-man's land between Kansu, Mongolia and Sinkiang, and promised by all accounts to be the hardest part of the whole journey. Actually we found the going on this stretch, though more rocky and mountainous, less difficult for the trucks to negotiate than the more sandy region between Suiyuan and the Etsin Gol. Our route on this second lap lay along the main camel trail followed by Lattimore, Sven Hedin and other foreign travellers of recent years. But the Gobi and the marches of Mongolia remain inadequately mapped, and this region, from the Etsin Gol to Ming-shui on the Turkistan frontier, is still blank on the one-to-four-million map of Asia, the best existing British map. Sven Hedin and his topographers must have filled in many of these blanks, but their work has not, so far as I am aware, been published yet in England.

* * *

Our two heavily laden trucks rolled smoothly over the firm, level desert westwards from the Etsin Gol. Now that we were at last clear of Ulan-chonchi and its rather dismal neighbourhood, I felt in better spirits and more confident that we should get safely through to Chinese Turkistan. For one thing we now had all our petrol with us, enough to reach Kashgar ; for another we had safely passed the various obstacles of the Etsin Gol ; and that without receiving from the wireless station there any disconcerting news from either Urumchi or Peking ; and, with 800 miles of desert travel behind us, the whole party had learned to know themselves and how to deal with the routine and the emergencies of life on the Gobi trail.

Thirty-five miles out we passed a well, called Luts'ao Ching. From here westwards there are no wells for a distance of ninety to a hundred miles. Mr. Lattimore,[1] travelling the road with camels, describes the hardships of " The Four Dry Stages," as they are known to the cameleers. It was a grim and desolate region, with the trail marked by an endless succession of skeletons of camels, each one a tragic story of thirst, exhaustion and collapse. But for us, travellers by motor-truck, the Four Dry Stages held no terrors—as long as things went well. Carrying our own supply of water, we could in half an hour turn any corner of the forbidding Gobi into a comfortable camp. All we needed was the dead tamarisk for fuel ; and Serat always knew by instinct or experience where this was or was not likely to be found.

Farther on the trail grew worse, ascending through

[1] *The Desert Road to Turkistan*, by Owen Lattimore.

the customary landscape of grotesquely shaped and coloured hills, some of which bore strange resemblance to mining tips and heaps of slag ; and we were all relieved to reach the well of Shih-pan Ching (" The Stone Slab Well "), the end of the Four Dry Stages, tucked away in the hills near the summit of the range.

Then down again into a broad depression of sand and gravel, a scene of horrid desolation, with many steep and stony gullies to be crossed on bottom gear. I know not why, but I recall each detail of the scene and how I lunched off cold sheep's liver and Thermos-heated coffee and buttered bread and honey, eaten standing by the trucks ; but how good it was ! Then more mountains, crossed by a rocky pass near Yeh-ma Ching, " The Well of the Wild Horse," apt name for so wild and desolate a spot. To the south there now came into view a range of higher mountains, which remained with us for some time, the Ma Tsung Shan. One could imagine that they resembled in their shape a horse's mane, which is the meaning of their Chinese name. The Hardt-Citroen expedition followed from Suchou to Mingshui a camel trail which took them through this range. They found a region of rich pastures, abundant water, the haunt of ibex and gazelle, mountain sheep, the wild horse and wild ass. Crossing the desolation of the Black Gobi by the main camel trail one would not suspect the existence of so agreeable a region near at hand. The Western Gobi desert has many secrets yet to be explored. Wild horses and wild camels are said to exist in this neighbourhood. We saw no direct evidence of either. The wild ass is common and is often, with characteristic Chinese lack of accuracy, referred to as *Yeh Ma* ("wild horse"), which may explain the name of Yeh-ma Ching.

*   *   *

On October 19 we made an early start, hoping to do a long day's journey on a better trail. We were now 4,000 feet or more above the sea, threading our way through stony ranges with sandy valleys in between ; now struggling up the rock-strewn slopes, now plunging heavily through sand, now bowling in fine style across smooth glacis of firm gravel. In two and a half hours we had travelled thirty miles, a rate of progress well above the average. But on the Gobi motor trail one never knows what the next moment may bring forth. We reached a well called Huo-shao Ching, a horrid spot, the ground covered with white alkali and a well of evil-smelling, bitter water. As we rested and smoked a cigarette before proceeding on our way, one of the men exclaimed and pointed at the old truck, which, we saw with consternation, had lost one of its rear spring brackets, so that the spring end hung lopsidedly and unsupported in the air. It took us some hours' work to effect a makeshift and provisional repair, enabling us to carry on and reach the same evening the sweet water spring at Kung-po Ch'uan. This was truck *Edsel's* second serious collapse.

At Kung-po Ch'uan [1] we found two yurts and two mud huts, housing a depot of the Sin-sui company and a tax station. The water from the spring was sweet and good and round about grew reedy

[1] *Ch'uan* or *Ch'uan-tzu* means in Chinese a sweet water spring ; *Ching* or *Ching-tzu* means a well, the water of which in the Gobi is often foul and bitter. The Mongol name for Kung-po Ch'uan is Bayin Buluk, meaning "The Copious Spring."

grass and camel scrub, dead at this season of the year but showing that in summer the place is almost an oasis and doubtless quite a pleasant spot. Our route here crossed a trail from south to north, connecting An-hsi (" City of Western Peace ") in Kansu with Uliasutai and Urga ; and the tax station, a new addition to the burdens of the camel caravans, had, we were told, been established at this point by the authorities of Kansu Province after they had had to surrender the Ulan-chonchi tax station to the new Inner Mongol Government at Pai-ling Miao. The caravan trade of China's borderlands is an unending struggle between the merchant and the tax collector.

*   *   *

As we approached the spring of Kung-po Ch'uan across a level plain we saw, while still a long way off, the keep and buildings of a castle prominently situated on a hill above the little settlement ; a sight which drew and held attention, for we had seen no buildings worthy of the name since leaving Pai-ling Miao. As we came closer we could see that the fortress, which looked so imposing from a long way off, was but a crumbling ruin ; all that remained of the stronghold of the Mongol monk who, a few years since, had terrorized the Gobi caravans from far and near. Innumerable legends and stories attach to this man of mystery. I was told he was a Kalmuck Mongol from Russian territory, a masterful man of fierce passions, said to have been endowed with supernatural powers, who, after a long career in the stormy politics of Central Asia, established himself in this no-man's land of the Black Gobi in the early nineteen-twenties, when war and rapine raged throughout Mongolia in the backwash of the Russian revolution and the struggle between Whites and Reds. There were strange happenings in Mongolia in those days of turmoil, but none stranger than the stories told of the career and exploits of this outlaw lama chief. For three years or so he ruled the Western Gobi, levying tribute on the passing caravans and raiding the surrounding desert far and wide. Eventually the Russians and the Outer Mongols took the affair in hand ; and the lama of the Black Gobi was killed in his fort at Kung-po Ch'uan and his followers dispersed. But his influence still pervades the neighbourhood and his story is endlessly discussed round the camp fires of passing caravans.

A number of European travellers have written in their books about the mysterious lama of the Black Gobi. Ossendowski, who was in Mongolia as a refugee from Siberia in 1921, actually met him and witnessed a demonstration of his hypnotic powers ; in Ossendowski's remarkable book he is named *Tushegoun Lama*. Owen Lattimore calls him *Chia Lama* (" The False Lama "). The Russian traveller Roerich, who passed through Kung-po Ch'uan on his way from Urga to Tibet, writes about him under the names of *Ja Lama*, *Ten-pei Jal-tsen*, *Pal-den* and *Nomun Khan Hutuktu*. Haslund, who came this way with Sven Hedin's camels, calls him *Dambin Jansang* and publishes his photograph, on which he is named in Chinese characters *No-yin Lama*. The Hungarian Geleta, who lived in Outer Mongolia for some years after the War, writes about him as *Dja Lama*. Roerich and others give an account of his extraordinary career, in the course of which he is said to have resided in Russia, Tibet, India, China and Mongolia. He was imprisoned in Russia, studied in the Drepung monastery in Lhasa, served in the Hutuktu's yamen in Peking, and was known and feared throughout Mongolia as long ago as the 'nineties of last century. He was one of the leaders of the Mongols at the time they revolted against China in 1912, later became ruler of Kobdo and Western Mongolia, and was again in the field against the Chinese in 1920. Later he fought against the Bolsheviks, and it was when the reds assumed control over Outer Mongolia that he withdrew into the no-man's land of the Black Gobi and ruled the desert from his fort at Kung-po Ch'uan. All the versions of the story agree about his supernatural (and presumably hypnotic) powers and emphasize his cruel and bloodthirsty character.[1]

After we had camped I walked up to the hill and viewed the ruins, an eerie and ill-omened spot. The sun was setting behind the desert mountains to the west ; the place seemed haunted by its past of ill repute and inexpressibly remote ; and I was glad to hurry down the hill and back to camp.

* * *

We had been gradually ascending all the way from the oasis of the Etsin Gol and at Kung-po Ch'uan we were already more than five thousand feet above the sea. We still continued to ascend, entering a range of mountains, haunt of wild ass and antelope. Crossing the pass we descended into a plain between two Gobi ranges, at the farther end of which, guard-

[1] See *Beasts, Men and Gods*, by Ossendowski ; *The Desert Road to Turkistan*, by Lattimore ; *Trails to Inmost Asia*, by Roerich ; *Men and Gods in Mongolia*, by Haslund ; and *The New Mongolia*, by Geleta. (The latter confuses the Lama's rule at Kobdo with his exploits and end in the Black Gobi.)

ing the entrance to the hills, we found the sand-blown ruins of a very ancient fort, and then some towers, marking the frontier of Chinese Turkistan.

This moment, the arrival at the border of the promised (or forbidden) land, had been much in my thoughts, since we knew not what sort of a reception to expect. We entered a ravine and came to Ming-shui (" Clear Water "), a ruined, roofless hut and spring, the name that marks the frontier line. I looked for soldiers, passport inspection, customs post and frontier guards. But the virgin desolation of the Gobi was unmarked by any sign of human life ; the empty desert, encircling wild and barren hills, the ruined hut, and nothing else.

The main lines of traffic between China and Turkistan converge from each direction to pass through two points, or rather mountain passages, called Hsing-hsing-hsia (" The Starry Defile "), on the cart road from Kansu, and Ming-shui (" Clear Water "), on the Mongolian camel trail. Rarely do caravans to or from China leave or enter Sinkiang by any other route. Both these points are marked on modern maps and from now on we were again on well-mapped ground.

We continued through flat valleys, passing the junction of our route with the camel trail to Barkul on the T'ien Shan's northern face. It is sometimes difficult in this maze of Gobi mountains, basins, plains and valleys, which seem thrown together any-how without regard to watersheds and ranges, to know whether one is going up or down. Actually we were still ascending, and nine miles from Ming-shui we reached another pass, six to seven thousand feet above the sea, over the main ridge separating Mongolia from Sinkiang. From this point began the long descent into the desert plains of Turkistan ; and here we had our first and memorable glimpse of the snows of the T'ien Shan, " The Celestial Mountains," which signal to the weary Gobi caravans the nearing of their journey's end.

These snow-capped summits, hanging in the air above the desert haze, are those of the Karlik Tagh, as the Turkis call the eastern end of the T'ien Shan overlooking Hami.

In this neighbourhood we met, or rather passed, a man hunched on a camel in his sheepskin robe, the first human being we had seen on the road since leaving the oasis of the Etsin Gol. He turned out to be an emissary of the tax station at Kung-po Ch'uan, sent out to spy for camel caravans from Sinkiang. He told us of a spring near by, where we made our first camp in Chinese Turkistan.

*   *   *

It was the twenty-first of October and at this still considerable height the Gobi winter was beginning to announce itself. That morning, when we hoped to make an early start, we were held up for an hour or more by the refusal of one of the engines to fire. Finally we took the carburettor down and found embedded in it a fair-sized lump of ice. This being removed, the trucks were quickly on the road again. We met with the same trouble often later on. Our petrol, packed in drums instead of tins the better to withstand the bumps and knocks of camel transport, contained water and other foreign substances. Fumbling with icy fingers to open up and clean the frozen carburettors in the bitter cold, we called down imprecations on the suppliers of that " gas." Petrol is the life blood of the motor caravan, and it cannot

Near the Well of the Wild Horse, Western Gobi

Near the Well of the Wild Horse, Western Gobi

Fort of Dja Lama at Kung-po Ch'uan in the Black Gobi

Ming-shui, on the Frontier of Mongolia and Chinese Turkistan

Lunch Halt
Photo by Serat and Kua Shu-ming

Serat Loading Up
Photo by Serat and Kua Shu-ming

Liu Taot'ai, General Yulbaz and Author at Hami

Mosque at the Tomb of the Princes of Hami

be too pure and good ; though one *can* make shift with almost anything that may be labelled " gas " ; including even kerosene.

Leaving our camp we topped some rising ground and saw in front of us displayed full-length the snow-capped massif of the Karlik Tagh, down to the base of which from where we stood there spread a vast expanse of gravel desert. Down this slope we sped at a tremendous pace, across the longest stretch of smooth firm surface we had yet encountered on the road. We passed some springs, with vegetation, where we surprised the antelope quite close drinking at water-holes. We passed a huge caravan, China bound, grazing far-flung on the surrounding desert scrub [1] ; and in the middle distance watching them two figures on their camels motionless ; colleagues of our friend the scout from Kung-po Ch'uan, watching the caravan to see that it should not escape the meshes of the tax collector's net.

We bore left-handed of the Karlik Tagh, which marks the eastern end of the great T'ien Shan range. An isolated hill served as a landmark far ahead. As we drew closer we distinguished trees, the straight and graceful Central Asian poplars, a mosque and houses. We had reached the first oasis and Turki settlement, called Miao-erh-ku, in Chinese Turkistan.

Again I looked for frontier post and guards. The farms and houses lay in ruins and when we pitched our camp there seemed no sign of life. Then there appeared two men, a woman and some children, our first *Ch'an-t'ou*,[2] all pitifully poor. At first the lan-

---

[1] The Gobi camel caravans graze all the morning, travelling in the afternoons and late into the night.

[2] *Ch'an-t'ou*, " Turban-heads," the Chinese name for the Turkis.

6

guage difficulty delayed an understanding. Our party could by its constitution readily converse on equal terms with Mongols or Chinese. But for Turki we depended on the few simple words and sentences which Serat and Chomcha had picked up during their stay the year before in Sinkiang. We explained ourselves as best we could, and the Turki villagers were soon on friendly terms and busy fetching food and fuel. But the oasis had been destroyed in the rebellion and there was hardly anything to be obtained.

*　　*　　*

On October 22 we covered the remaining fifty-six miles to Hami by a fair road, except for some heavy sand round I-k'o-shu. Here, where we found trees and cultivated fields, the outskirts of the big Hami oasis, our route ran into the main cart road from Kansu, marked by an endless succession of telegraph poles stretching to the horizon either way. But this famous land-line, which used to run 3,000 miles across the deserts of Central Asia, linking Peking with Urumchi and Kashgar, was derelict, the wire, where it remained at all, hanging in festoons along the ground. The line was destroyed in the rebellion ; and now the local Government of Sinkiang prefer to control their own telegraphic communications by means of wireless.

In this neighbourhood we saw for the first time the system of underground irrigation channels, which is a feature of oasis life in many parts of Chinese Turkistan. Outwardly all that one sees is what appears to be a line of wells stretching across the desert. These wells are connected underground with one another on ground sloping down from the moun-

tains into the desert plain ; so that finally at the
end of the line an unfailing supply of water runs out
into the open to water the oases, which lie in the
desert some distance from the Karlik Tagh. The
labour involved in digging this artificial underground
irrigation system must have been enormous ; and
the Turkis are a lazy people compared with the
industrious Chinese. But, once built, the subterranean irrigation channels, fed by the mountain
springs and snows, can be relied on to produce an
unfailing supply of pure, sweet water, which turns
the barren desert into smiling fields and gardens of
cotton, corn and fruit.[1]

*　　*　　*

Hami, called Kumul by the Turkis, was one of
the old native kingdoms of Eastern Turkistan and
the last to lose its independent status. Its mediatized
rulers retained until 1930 a measure of autonomy.
In that year the last ruling Prince, Shah Maksud,
died, and the Chinese authorities from Urumchi
proceeded to take over the control of the local
administration. It was this Chinese interference
with the native rulers of Hami that provoked the
Turki rising, which led in turn to the Tungan invasion
from Kansu and the Moslem war. The oasis is one
of the largest and most favoured in Chinese Turkistan
and used to enjoy a big caravan trade with China.
The Hami melons are considered by the Chinese the
best in the world and supplies used regularly to be
sent by the local princes as tribute to the Manchu
court in Peking. Politically Hami has always

[1] The same system of underground irrigation by *Karez* is
found right across Central Asia to Persia and Baluchistan.

been, and still is, the eastern gateway to Chinese Turkistan.

* * *

As we advanced through the Hami oasis I looked out anxiously for any sign of the nature of the reception, good or bad, in store for us. At last, a mile or two from the city walls, we met a motor-truck, crammed with soldiers and civilians, Chinese and Turkis, who turned out to be the local notables, followed by another truck, more soldiers, and General Yulbaz, the military potentate of Hami. We all stopped, descended and exchanged appropriate courtesies. Then on again, first the truck-load of soldiers and officials, then Yulbaz, then our party ; and, so processing, we entered Hami, beflagged in honour of our arrival, and crowds of welcoming Turkis in the streets. I felt embarrassed by the cordiality of our reception ; having indeed expected just the opposite, in view of the difficulties raised before the journey's start ; and my mind dwelled on the contrast between our arrival and that of other recent European travellers,[1] whose introduction at Hami to Chinese Turkistan had been a nightmare of warring Tungans, Turkis and Chinese, rifle and machine-gun fire, decapitations, burning villages and hairbreadth escapes from violence and death. Fortunately the times had changed and peace, by Chinese standards, was again restored.

We drove to the rooms assigned to us in the *Taot'ai's* yamen, comfortable quarters, thickly carpeted in Turki style. Later all assembled, engaged in small talk and partook of refreshments, tea, Hami fruits,

[1] See the adventures of the Hardt-Citroen and Sven Hedin expeditions as related in *An Eastern Odyssey* and *Big Horse's Flight*.

and Russian sugar, sweets and cigarettes. These products of the Soviet Union met us at every turn throughout our stay in Sinkiang ; the sugar was good ; the cigarettes but ghosts of the good Russian *papyrossi* of pre-war days. The *Taot'ai*,[1] Mr. Liu Ying-lin was a Chinese from Kansu whom I had met in that province many years before. And amongst the other officials was a Mr. Wan Hsien-ping, from the Foreign Department at Urumchi, sent by the Tupan,[2] with two trucks of soldiers, to welcome and escort us to the provincial capital.

* * *

We stayed two days in Hami, being entertained by our joint hosts, the Turki general, Yulbaz, and the Chinese Taot'ai, Liu, representing the new con-dominium, which we were to meet throughout the province, of Chinese-Turki rule. Their hospitality was overwhelming and a foretaste of the treatment accorded to us all through our stay in Sinkiang. General Yulbaz himself, a bearded Turki past middle age, was a charming host. He had been a prominent figure at Hami for many years, from the time of the old Prince, Shah Maksud, whose death in 1930 preceded the recent rebellion. Yulbaz had in fact been one of the leaders of the Turkis of Hami in the

[1] In Sinkiang the *Taot'ai* (" Intendant of Circuit ") is nowa-days called *Hsing-cheng-chang* (" Head of the Executive Adminis-tration "), but I have retained the term *Taot'ai*, which is still used colloquially, as simpler and better known. In China Proper the *Taot'ai* has been abolished, the unit of administration being the *Hsien* (" District ").

[2] The term *Tupan* (pronounced *Dooban*), which is not at present used in China Proper, means the equivalent of Military Governor as applied to the head of the Government of Chinese Turkistan.

original troubles. But in the years of confusion and fighting that followed he, and the Turkis in general, had gone over to the Chinese side. Yulbaz was now the Big Man of Hami, the eastern gateway to Chinese Turkistan. Both he and his soldiers looked best in Turki dress ; for there was something odd and incongruous about their Turki faces in Chinese military uniforms.

The next morning after breakfast, reinforced by a jug of rich fresh milk, we went out for a sightseeing tour on horseback : myself ; General Yulbaz, an imposing figure with his full beard, military uniform and well-accoutred mount ; Liu *Taot'ai*, wearing a cap of astrakhan and the appearance of aloof refinement bred by two thousand years of culture into the Chinese gentleman ; Mr. Wan, in owlish spectacles, no horseman, but an agreeable young man of the new student type ; and an escort of soldiers, military officers and small officials. We rode fine, upstanding ponies from Karashar, reputed to be the home of the best horse-flesh of Turkistan, on Andijani saddles ; these have high pommels and relatively broad and comfortable seats and are a great improvement on the narrow Chinese and Mongolian saddles to ride on which is torture to the European or anyone without the posterior anatomy of a native of the farther East. The party ambled and cantered along through clouds of dust, while all the Turkis by the roadside salaamed to the General. We visited the various local sights, the tombs of the Hami Princes, the ruins of the palace, the principal mosques, a Chinese temple called the Lung Wang Miao, which, held by the rebels, had been totally destroyed, and the *Chiu Lung Shu* (" Nine Dragon Tree "), the latter a famous curiosity to all Chinese, nine venerable

86

willows growing out of one root, but, like most of Hami, destroyed in the hostilities.

Hami consists of three walled cities : the Old City, where we were quartered in the *Taot'ai's* yamen ; the Moslem City, containing the ruined palaces ; and the New City, which used to be the Chinese citadel and now housed the Turki troops of Yulbaz. Ruins everywhere ; the Chinese had held the place against the attacks of Tungans, Turkis and Kazaks ; and the suburbs and most of the Moslem city had been reduced to heaps of rubble.

Two banquets, one with Liu *Taot'ai* and the other with the General, occupied the rest of a busy day. The food was mainly Chinese fare, with all the customary delicacies, imported from Tientsin by caravan and Sin-sui truck, and mutton pilaus to meet the Turki taste. But in place of Chinese wine (the golden *Shao-hsing Chiu*, than which there is no healthier form of alcohol), we drank a variety of Russian cherry, cranberry, and other brandies, labelled, in English lettering, *Savin Trust U.S.S.R.*, strong, sweet and oily to the taste. The General, in Turki skull-cap, in place of his Chinese military headgear, presided benevolently at the feast.

At Hami we first met the paper currency of Sinkiang—*tael* notes of the poorest manufacture, exchanging locally at thirty-six to forty fifty-*tael* notes for one Chinese silver dollar. As the *tael* used to be a weight of silver worth a dollar and a third, the depreciation had been considerable. We had brought with us Chinese silver dollars from the coast and found them everywhere in great demand. But exchange operations had to be conducted tactfully ; since the official rate, enforced by proclamation under pain of condign punishment, was very different to that obtainable in the bazaar. To add to the general confusion of the currency of Sinkiang, the Chinese Government during our stay in Turkistan abolished altogether the Chinese silver dollar, replacing them with dollar notes worth only half as much ; but we remained in ignorance of this astonishing development and continued bartering our siver dollars for sackfuls of the local notes of Turkistan.

CHAPTER VI

ACROSS THE T'IEN SHAN TO URUMCHI

Departure from Hami—A Turki meal—Russian motor
trucks in Sinkiang—Turki bread—Into the T'ien Shan—
Fort of Ch'i-ku Chingtzu—Ta Shih-t'ou Pass—Kazaks—
Plains of Dzungaria—Arrival in Muli Ho—Kuch'eng—
Another riding party—Kuch'eng to Urumchi—Devas-
tation of the Moslem rebellion—Arrival in Urumchi.

WE left Hami on October 24. Black clouds shrouded
the Karlik Tagh and a gentle rain was falling. It
seemed to be our fate to meet abnormal weather
everywhere ; for rain was, we were told, a rare
phenomenon in Hami. The track through the oasis
was slippery and bad in places, but nothing compared
to our experiences of bad going in the Gobi.

We made an imposing procession as we trundled
out of Hami. First Mr. Wan's truck, with himself
and his escort of Chinese soldiers from Urumchi ;
then our two trucks ; and, behind us, the second
Urumchi truck, and a truck-load of Turki braves
sent by General Yulbaz to escort us out of his
jurisdiction.

The General himself and Liu *Taot'ai* accompanied
us for more than thirty miles to the hamlet of Sanp'u
("Third Village"), where they entertained me to a
farewell lunch in the house of the local Turki headman. This was my first real Turki meal and a very
good one too. When we first sat down, reclining on
cushions on the carpeted *k'ang*,[1] we were faced with

[1] A Chinese word meaning the raised platform filling up half
of a room in a Chinese or Turki house on which one sits, eats and
sleeps.

89

small tables loaded with good Turki bread, cold snacks and sweets. Being hungry, I made a good meal and got up to go—only to be informed that the meal itself had not yet begun ! Whereupon an enormous dish of steaming pilau, chicken, mutton, rice and fat, was brought in and placed before us. We all set to with our fingers ; and I admired and did my best to imitate the General's technique and the skill with which he flicked into his mouth handfuls of greasy rice and meat. Liu *Taot'ai* and Mr. Wan dealt with the pilau, like myself, as amateurs and were relatively inexpert. The Chinese word for pilau is *chua-fan* ; the characters meaning " rice that is grabbed at with the hand." The world is divided up amongst peoples who eat with knives and forks, with chopsticks, and with their fingers ; it is a question whether the chopsticks are not the more refined and delicate of the three sets of implements.

Lunch over we made our final farewells and proceeded on our way. The road, a cart track and relatively good, lay north of west across the desert with the snowclad Karlik Tagh on our right-hand side. Nearly everywhere in Sinkiang we followed the cart tracks, which, on the whole, afforded better going than the camel trails of the Gobi. The high-wheeled carts of Turkistan, called *arba*, have a broader gauge than the carts of China and this greatly facilitates the use of the roads by motor traffic ; since, wherever a cart can go, a motor-car can probably follow ; whereas in China a cart track will nearly always, sooner or later, become too narrow for a motor vehicle to pass.

We were now travelling under official auspices, personally conducted by Mr. Wan, to whom were left all the arrangements as regards lodging and supplies. The free-and-easy life on the desert trail was over, our little Mongol tents, which had furnished us with warmth and shelter for so many nights, remained packed up, and accommodation, good, indifferent and bad, in yamens and caravanserais, was from now on always found for us in Chinese Turkistan. It is unnecessary, travelling by motor-truck, to carry tents on the main roads of Sinkiang ; though one must be prepared at times for very rough accommodation ; especially since the destruction in the last rebellion of so many posting stages, villages and serais.

* * *

Our first night was spent at San-tao-lingtzu, one of many ruined Turki hamlets, fifty miles from Hami. We were there by two o'clock, and might have doubled our day's journey ; but, quarters having been prepared, sheep slaughtered and all arrangements made, we settled in. We seemed, in contrast to the silences of our Gobi camps, to be a noisy crowd, my own men, Chinese and Turki soldiers, local villagers, and drivers and mechanics of the Russian motor-trucks. Two of these were Russians, White refugees or Red adventurers—the two types are now merged in Chinese Turkistan. Their trucks were Russian *Amo* vehicles, a mass production of the Soviet State, with which I was to become well acquainted during the next few weeks ; for these *Amo* trucks constitute almost the entire motor transport of Chinese Turkistan, which is a monopoly of the local Government. I suppose there must, at the time of our visit, have been some hundreds of them, probably supplied by the authorities of the U.S.S.R. as part of some general arrangement under which the Russians lent their benevolent assistance, in return for value received or later due, to the Urumchi Government. They seemed to be useful vehicles, strongly constructed, and built to carry heavy loads ; but under-engined for their weight and less efficient than our Fords. Whether the frequent small mechanical troubles from which they suffered were due to faults in the trucks or in their handling, I should not like to say. The Russian petrol too was probably much inferior to ours.

The European who reaches Sinkiang from China will appreciate the good Turki bread. The Chinese do not bake bread and in the interior of China no bread worthy of the name can be obtained, so that the traveller must either make his own, with baking powder, or go without. In the desert on the way nothing is in any case obtainable. But, once arrived in Turkistan, in every town or village one can buy, for the equivalent of a fraction of a farthing, excellent bread, fresh baked, in the form of small circular loaves with a hole in the centre, of which we daily consumed large quantities.

*　　*　　*

On the second day we began to work into the mountains, gradually ascending. On our right there still rose the main range of the T'ien Shan ; on our left the ground fell away into the boundless desert, a region, I was told, of terrible winds and sandstorms, which have annihilated many caravans. A short cut to Turfan lies that way, a risky road. We were following the old Imperial highway to Urumchi and Dzungaria, along which countless travellers from earliest Central Asian days have wound their weary way. It is divided up into posting stages, each marked by a group of huts round well or spring, to be covered between dawn and dusk by carts or caravans. To-day the motor-truck lumbers past half a dozen of them in the day. Most of the posting stations were in ruins, part of the trail of desolation left by the last Mohammedan rebellion. The road in the mountains was still relatively good, past I-wan Ch'uan (" One Cup Spring ") and Ch'ê Ku-lu Ch'uan (" Cart Wheel Spring "), both posting stations totally destroyed, whence we descended through queer Gobi hills of grey and purple to reach a broad, sandy basin and a ruined fort, called Ch'i-ku Chingtzu (or Ch'i-chüeh Chingtzu, " The Well of the Seven Horns, or Corners "). Inside the fort were heaps of rubble, remains of camels and other animals, dust, sand and battle rubbish, and one house, in which we spent the night. The place lies at the bifurcation of the roads to Turfan and Urumchi and had been the scene of much fierce fighting between the Moslem Tungans and Chinese. It was near Ch'i-ku Chingtzu that the the young German, Von Hanneken, a name well and honourably known in Tientsin and the North China Treaty Ports, had disappeared a few years since. He set out from Hami during the rebellion to travel to Urumchi and was never seen again. The Chinese say he was killed by Kazak robbers in the neighbouring ranges of the T'ien Shan.

* * *

The next day we covered more than eighty miles to Mu-li Ho. Mr. Wan warned us to expect a hard day, since we had to cross the main range of the T'ien Shan, and to keep well together, as there were " bad men," *Ha-sa* (Kazaks), about in the hills.

Winter was approaching in these Asiatic highlands,

and there were fourteen degrees of frost when we started up the trucks, after some delay with frozen water in the carburettors. We soon entered the mountains and followed up a winding gorge. The road was rocky, but, all things considered, very good. We arrived at the ruined posting station of Ta Shih-t'ou (" Big Rock "), where our escort of Turki braves left us to return to Hami. They were a decent lot of men and well behaved ; but I fancy that, had we had far to go together, there might have been trouble between the Turki soldiers and our Urumchi escort of Manchurians.

Ta Shih-t'ou was a bleak and desolate spot, the surrounding mountains already patched with snow. A mile beyond we reached the pass, and realized with satisfaction that we had crossed the formidable barrier of the Celestial Mountains. The pass is, in fact, a very easy one, only 6,700 feet above the sea, across a gap in the main range between the snows of the Karlik Tagh and those of Bogdo Ula.

Beyond the pass, instead of immediately descending, we entered on a plateau country of flat valleys, home of the Kazak, parties of whom we met, shifting their camps and flocks and herds to lower winter pasturages. The Kazak must, I suppose, be first cousins to the Kirghiz ; both are nomad Turks, who graze their sheep and cattle in the ranges of the T'ien Shan, the former in the north and the latter in the south of Turkistan.

Farther on the flat valleys opened out onto steppes of sandy grass, patched and sprinkled with snow, a rather dismal landscape. We had reached Dzungaria, the steppe country of Northern Turkistan lying between the T'ien Shan and the Altai mountains. This dreary-looking plain was one of the reservoirs from which the waves of nomad invasions, Huns, Turks and Mongols, poured east and west in olden times.

The snowy line of the Celestial Mountains lay now on our left-hand side ; and we were looking at its northern face, having crossed the main range by the gap of Ta Shih-t'ou. The road across the steppe was very good indeed and we rolled along mile after mile in top gear. At intervals of twenty miles or so were ruined posting stations. Rare carts lumbered across the snow-besprinkled plain, bound to or from Hami, Kuch'eng or Urumchi ; the passengers huddled in their sheepskins under the awnings of straw mats ; grim travelling in winter, with, at the end of a long day's journey, no shelter but a ruined, roofless inn. Two wolves, at which the Chinese soldiers fired without result, loped easily across our front.

The autumn day was drawing in as we rounded an outlying spur of the T'ien Shan and drove into Mu-li Ho, a small walled district city, mostly in ruins, the streets a sea of snow, slush and mud, and full of strange-looking Kazaks, Turks and Tartars. As we arrived three Russian *Amo* trucks drove in from Barkul, crashing through the narrow crowded streets, their blond Slav drivers contrasting sharply with the Central Asian types.

Here Mr. Wan's commissariat arrangements failed and our arrival created chaos, as we were not expected. We drove to the yamen, a group of tumbledown buildings in the last stages of dilapidation and very cold, where we were received by the embarrassed magistrate, a Sinkiang Chinese. I thought regretfully of our comfortable desert camps, where we depended on no one but ourselves. We must, I fear, have caused a sad disturbance in the routine of magisterial life at Mu-li Ho. But all things and situations come to their appointed end, and, somehow or other, we sorted ourselves out and settled in, myself in His Honour's one and only room, serving as office, bed-chamber and sitting-room.

The little town of Mu-li Ho lies at the foot of the T'ien Shan, on the banks of a clear stream, with trees and cultivation. It must have been, before the devastation of the Moslem war, a pleasant spot; but now, in early winter, it had a desolate and mournful air. The magistrate bemoaned its fate.

*　　*　　*

The next day a short morning's run across the level steppe brought us to Kuch'eng, now known officially as Ch'i-t'ai Hsien, revival of an ancient name. On our left hand lay the glittering wall of the Celestial Mountains. In all my considerable experience of Asiatic travel, I do not recall a range which so impresses one with its character as a barrier between two otherwise adjacent areas. The triple peaks of sacred Bogdo Ula, which overlook Urumchi, were already visible, towering above the rest. Yet in actual height, with peaks rising only some twelve to fifteen thousand feet above the sea, this portion of the T'ien Shan range is, by Asian standards, relatively insignificant.

Kuch'eng is not a Turki, but a Chinese city; the biggest Chinese trading centre in the whole of Sinkiang and the terminus of the caravan routes linking Turkistan with distant China. But the caravan trade was now moribund, and the Chinese merchants bitterly lamented the political conditions which had all but severed their communications with the China coast.

Our Host and Hostess at San-tao-lingtzu

Turki Escort Parading to Return from Ta Shih-t'ou

Fort of Ch'i-ku Chingtzu

Good Going in the Ta Shih-t'ou Gorge

Kazak in the T'ien Shan

Crossing the T'ien Shan, October 26

Approach of Winter

On the Road near Urumchi

In the afternoon another riding party was arranged, myself, Mr. Wan, the leading Chinese merchants and several military officers. In these parts, everyone must ride, even the stoutest Chinese merchant, to get from place to place. Again we cantered round in clouds of dust, admiring the local sights, such as they were. But Kuch'eng, as a Chinese commercial centre, has little of special interest to show the visitor ; some ancient sites, the Manchu city, yamens, and the Shansi Guild ; the latter with a fine pagoda, from the top of which one gets the best view of the town and, in the background, the snowy line of the Celestial Mountains. My mount was hard-mouthed, angular and fitted with a Russian cossack saddle ; and after two hours I had had enough and was relieved when we adjourned for a banquet to which we had been invited by the Chinese merchants ; good fellows all ; and, in this distant land, I always felt at home with Chinese faces round about. The only drawback to these Chinese feasts in Sinkiang was the absence of the good yellow wine of China ; in place of which we drank Russian brandies and other alcoholic Soviet concoctions, heady and sweet.

*　　*　　*

From Kuch'eng to Urumchi there were left but 126 miles, which we might, I think, have covered in one day. But as the *Tupan* wished to be apprised of our arrival, Mr. Wan arranged that we should travel easily and reach the capital on the morning of the second day. The road lay at first across the steppe, covered by melting snow and mud. (In winter-time this route is closed by snow, and motor traffic follows the southern Turfan road.) Farther on we passed through a series of oases, where the going was in places very bad. Here trees, hedges, fields and farms made up an almost European landscape ; a gamey-looking country-side, with many partridges.

We passed two district cities, Fu-yuan and Fu-k'ang Hsien ; tumbledown yamens, where the Chinese magistrates, as decrepit as their establishments, put themselves out to entertain the *Tupan's* visitor ; San-t'ai, the centre of a big oasis ; and Tzu-ni Ch'uantzu (" Muddy Spring "), well named ; for here one of the Russian trucks stuck in a bog-hole and had to be hauled out by one of Mr. Henry Ford's machines.

We met considerable traffic, Turks, Kazaks, Tartars, with faces of the Huns of ancient times, Chinese and here and there a Russian. The road was lined with ruins. The Tungan army had left a trail of desolation in the style traditional of Chinese Moslem wars. The old-time Chinese magistrate of Fu-k'ang told us of the sufferings of his flock in the rebellion. His district included the lower ranges of the Bogdo Ula group, with many Kazak. But the latter, he said, only made " small trouble " ; the " big trouble-makers came from outside " (a euphemistic reference to the Tungan host), and burned the Chinese farms and houses and massacred all the Chinese who could not escape by fleeing to the hills. This was the only part of Sinkiang where I saw Chinese settled on the land. But the Fu-k'ang magistrate told me that eight-tenths of his people were Moslems and only two-tenths Chinese.

Approaching Urumchi we struck the remains of a built motor road, which used to run part of the way from the capital to Kuch'eng. At the township of Ku-mu-ti we crossed a clear stream flowing down from Bogdo Ula, where, with an eye to our entrance into the capital, we drove up and down in the water to wash our mud-bespattered trucks, and got one badly stuck in the stream-bed for our pains. We passed through low hills, and there at last lay stretched before us our long-awaited destination, Urumchi, the capital of Chinese Turkistan. City of sinister repute, it looked a pleasant spot; grey city walls along a mountain stream, trees, cultivated fields and groves, surrounded by low hills and backed by the snows of the Celestial Mountains and the three majestic peaks of sacred Bogdo Ula.

A few miles outside the city we were met by a group of the leading officials, including Mr. Wang, the Mayor, and Mr. Ch'en, the local "Foreign Minister." And farther on I spied the jodhpurs and "Bombay bowlers" of two Anglo-Indian figures, Colonel and Mrs. Thomson Glover,[1] who had reached Urumchi some days earlier from Kashgar and had come out in the *Tupan's* motor-car, a neat Vauxhall saloon, to meet me. We greeted one another, feeling like Stanley and Dr. Livingstone, and drove together to the city. I had not spoken English since leaving Pai-ling Miao. Outside the walls another group awaited us, the young men of the China Inland Mission, courageous pioneers who live for years on end in utter isolation in this remote centre of High Tartary. With them were the Misses French and Cable, three famous Central Asian lady travellers, who had reached Urumchi recently from Russia.[2]

We drove to our quarters in the city, and as we parked the trucks outside, I looked at the speedometers; they marked 1,563 miles from Suiyuan.

[1] See page 22.
[2] Authors of *Through the Jade Gate and Central Asia*.

CHAPTER VII

WORK AND PLAY IN URUMCHI

Description of Urumchi—I join forces with Colonel
Thomson Glover—The *Tupan* and personalities of Chinese
Turkistan—Diplomatic discussions—Banquets—Celebration of the Soviet National Day—The Urumchi
Wireless Station and the *T'ien Shan Daily News*—The
foreign community and the C.I.M.—Excursions and
shooting parties—Preparations for departure.

URUMCHI is the Tartar or Mongolian name, which
usually appears on European maps, for the city known
to the Chinese as Tihwa, and colloquially to the
caravan men as Hung Miaotzu (" Red Temple "),
from a prominently situated Chinese temple in the
neighbourhood. In the Middle Ages it was known
as Bishbalik, when it was one of the chief cities of
the Uighurs, the pre-Mongol Turkish rulers of High
Tartary. At the time of the Emperor Ch'ien Lung's
conquests in Dzungaria early in the eighteenth century Urumchi became a Manchu-Chinese military
centre : and the descendants of the old Manchu
garrison are still found in the neighbourhood. It is
said that a knowledge of the Manchu tongue, formerly
used in Court circles in Peking but now to all intents
and purposes a dead language even in Manchuria,
survives amongst them. Since the establishment of
modern Sinkiang after the suppression of Yakub
Beg's rebellion in the eighties of last century, Urumchi
(Tihwa) has been the seat of the Chinese administration of the New Dominion.

The capital of Sinkiang is pleasantly situated along the banks of the Urumchi river, a clear mountain stream, on the northern face of the T'ien Shan. The best view of the city and its environs is obtained from the Red Temple pagoda, situated on a bluff overlooking the river outside the north-west corner of the walls. From here the eye sweeps round a circle of hills and mountains, with the grey city walls embowered in trees stretching along the river in the foreground. To the west and south-west are the ranges of the Celestial Mountains, with the main cart road to Manas, Ili and Chuguchak carried over a bridge across the river in the foreground ; to the south can be seen the gap in the mountains through which the South Road passes to Turfan, Karashar and Kashgar ; to the east the snows of the T'ien Shan are continued in the massif of Bogdo Ula, " The Holy Mountain," whose triple peaks overlook the scene ; to the north-east are ranges of foothills crossed by the cart road to Kuch'eng, Barkul and Hami ; and to the north the valley leads out on to the Dzungarian steppe, where the river is said to end in a vast marsh.

Urumchi comprises three separate towns, adjoining one another from north to south. First there is the main walled Chinese city, where the yamens and Chinese shops are situated ; here one might in places fancy oneself in any northern Chinese city. Adjoining lies the walled Moslem city, with Turki and Tartar bazaars, entering which one steps at a stride into the heart of Central Asia. Continuing south, one goes out through the Moslem city into the Nan Kuan (" Southern Suburb "), the Russian quarter, resembling a small Siberian town, with Russian shops and houses and the compound of the Soviet

Consulate. The Chinese and Moslem cities are quite small, only three-quarters of a mile or so across ; while the Russian settlement is a narrow strip a mile or two in length. The shops in the Chinese city seemed to me well stocked, and I was surprised, in view of the difficulties of trade with China, to see so many Chinese goods displayed, hosiery, cigarettes, tinned foods and Chinese and foreign sundries. Chinese trade resembles the flow of water, and will trickle through the smallest crevice in the dam.

Our stay in Urumchi lasted from the end of October to the middle of November. When we arrived it was still autumn ; by the time we left winter had closed its grip on the Dzungarian plain, the countryside was snowbound and the thermometer had already fallen to zero Fahrenheit. From our short experience of the place in November, I should say that the winter climate must be exceedingly severe ; the local Chinese, many of whom came from the Three Eastern Provinces, told me it resembled that of North Manchuria.

That there is something gloomy, dark and sinister about the Urumchi atmosphere no one who has resided there is likely to deny. To what extent this atmosphere is due to, or has been aggravated by, the Russian influence, is more debatable. For I fancy it existed before the introduction of recent years of Russian methods into the local government. It may be partly due to a feeling of being in a trap ; it has for years been notorious that, difficult as it may be to reach Urumchi, it is often far more difficult to get away again. All sorts of visitors and foreign residents—mainly, but not only, Russians—have been detained for months and sometimes years waiting for passports which would enable them to leave. Others have known the inside of the Urumchi prison ; a place of evil reputation, even for prisons.

*   *   *

I had now joined forces with Colonel Thomson Glover, who, accompanied by his wife, had travelled up from his post at Kashgar by Russian motor-truck, placed at his disposal by the local Government. This enabled them to cover in two weeks a journey through Eastern Turkistan that normally occupies as many months by cart and pony. It was, in the prevailing atmosphere of rebellion, suspicion and unrest, a plucky journey for a lady to undertake. But Mrs. Thomson Glover is one of the world's courageous women, plays a good game of polo, and is an intrepid traveller not likely to be daunted by the hardships and discomforts of a journey through Turkistan.

We were all quartered together in the Foreign Bureau, a semi-foreign building, with lofty inter-communicating rooms in the Russian style, heated by big Russian corner stoves. Here we were entertained as the guests of the Provincial Government. We were indeed most comfortably lodged. Attached to us, for our convenience and entertainment while in Urumchi, was a young Chinese secretary of the local Government, Mr. Paul Bien, from Peking, who was unremitting in looking after us and facilitating our official labours. Our respective staffs made a picturesque assemblage of Central Asian types, my two Mongols and four Chinese, and Colonel Thomson Glover's Indians, Kashmiris and Turki followers from Kashgar. Between us we commanded most of the local languages, excepting Russian, of which I have but a smattering.

*   *   *

Our first day in the capital was taken up with official calls on General Sheng Shih-ts'ai, the *Tupan* (Military Governor), Mr. Li Jung, the *Chu-hsi* (Civil Governor), and the leading officials of the Government of Chinese Turkistan. The General's full title was *Pien-fang Tu-pan*, which may be translated "High Commissioner for Frontier Defence." *Chu-hsi* means "Chairman" or "President" (of the Provincial Government), and is the term now used in China to designate the President of the Government of China and the Chairmen of the Provincial Governments. This is all part of the committee system of government adapted by the Kuo-min-tang [1] from the Russian system. But these arrangements are not to be taken too seriously in China, where make-belief is one of the chief factors in the national life; and the *Chu-hsi*, or "Chairmen," of the Provincial Governments are in effect nothing but the former Governors under another name. Li *Chu-hsi* (Mr. Li Jung, the Chairman) should therefore have been the superior of Sheng *Tupan* (General Sheng, the Frontier Defence Commissioner); but this was another case where things Chinese must be assessed and judged by the facts rather than the names; and, while General Sheng was omnipotent, Mr. Li gave rather the impression of a figure-head.

General Sheng Shih-ts'ai, an alert-looking Chinese military officer in the early forties, received us in the big yamen. In this and subsequent conversations he told us frankly of his situation and the many difficulties he had to face. A native of Manchuria, he had served in the armies of Chang Tso-lin and Chang Hsueh-liang, and had been sent a few years since by the National Government in a military

[1] The ruling party in China.

General Sheng Shih-tsai, *Tupan* of Sinkiang

(*Chinese photo*)

capacity to Sinkiang. In 1933, when the Tungans were attacking Urumchi and the former Governor, Chin Shu-jen, was overthrown by a local *coup d'état*, Sheng Shih-ts'ai became by force of circumstance the *de facto* ruler of the province. As he himself was a Manchurian, and as at this juncture the forces of the local Government were reinforced by the timely arrival of the Chinese troops expelled from Manchuria by the Japanese, the administration of Sinkiang was, at the time of our visit in 1935, largely in the hands of a Manchurian faction. Sheng *Tupan* and these Manchurian troops, known locally as *Tung-pei Chün* (North-eastern Army), were, like all other Chinese from Manchuria, particularly incensed against Japan ; a circumstance which led them to accept all the more readily the assistance proffered by the Soviet.

The *Tupan* made a special point of explaining his attitude towards my mission and the reasons, concerned with my personal safety, which had led him at the outset to oppose my coming ; also his attitude towards the National Government at Nanking, to whom he professed his loyalty and full obedience. *But*, he had just emerged victorious from a life-and-death struggle with the Tungans and he owed nothing to Nanking, but much to Moscow, for the assistance which had enabled him to triumph over Ma Chung-ying.

Regarding the situation quite objectively, it is difficult to see what other line Nanking, or Sheng *Tupan*, could have adopted at the time. Both were the victims of capricious circumstance and the great distances separating Turkistan from China ; while the Soviet, with all the resources and implements of modern warfare, were close at hand.

The *Chu-hsi*, Li Jung, looked his part, that of the old-time Chinese scholar-mandarin, with long grey beard, Chinese horn spectacles, and dignified of mien. In conversation he indulged in platitudes and long harangues, delivered in the sonorous tones of a Chinese orator, about his own career, the history of Sinkiang, which had been left to fight its own battles without assistance from the Central Government, the high qualities of His Excellency the *Tupan*, and the prospects of peace and prosperity under the new régime. A native of Barkul, his Chinese had a Sinkiang brogue, which made it difficult at times to follow all he said ; whereas the *Tupan* and other officials from Manchuria spoke, as all Manchurians do, the clearest Pekinese.

The *Fu Chu-hsi*, Vice-Chairman of the Provincial Government, was the Turki leader Khoja Niaz, who had played a prominent part, with Yulbaz, in the original rising at Hami in 1931 and had later joined the Chinese side against the Tungans. Now, as *Fu Chu-hsi* and arrayed in Chinese uniform, he was the leading symbol of Chinese-Turki co-operation in the government of Turkistan. Yet his bearded Turki figure seemed incongruous and out of place against the Chinese background ; and, like many other Turkis, he had amongst his Chinese colleagues a rather melancholy look. Since I could not speak the Turki language, I was not able to make his acquaintance beyond the most formal intercourse. As the acknowledged leader of the Turki people, Khoja Niaz was an interesting figure, and I was sorry not to have had the opportunity of learning more about him.[1]

The Chinese, with their clumsy monosyllabic lan-

[1] The *Khojas* were, up to the time of the Manchu conquest, the hereditary native rulers of Turkistan.

guage, petrified in written characters which date from the dawn of history, have as much trouble with Turki as with European names. Khoja Niaz appears in Chinese as Ho-Chia-Ni-Ya-Tzu ; Yulbaz as Yao-Lo-Po-Shih. At the end of the Great War all China rang with the name of Wei-Li-Sun ; which only the initiated foreigner would recognize as that of Mr. Wilson, President of the U.S.A.

The other leading officials in the local Government were the Commissioners for Foreign Affairs and Finance, Education, Industry and Reconstruction, the Mayor and the *Taot'ai*. They and their principal subordinates were either old-time officials of Sinkiang or new-comers from Manchuria, with a sprinkling of Turkis to maintain the principle of joint Chinese-Turki rule. But control rested in the hands of the Chinese and their Russian advisers. The official with whom Colonel Thomson Glover and I carried on our diplomatic conversations was Mr. Ch'en Tê-li, who duplicated the posts of Commissioner for Foreign Affairs and Finance and was therefore the busiest man in Urumchi. We were in his yamen nearly every day and usually found his ante-rooms crowded with Chinese callers, Russian advisers and other visitors.

Mr. Ch'en was small, pale and frail-looking, but had all the chauvinism, mental agility and tenacity of purpose with which Chinese officials of his type are often so liberally endowed. Colonel Thomson Glover is also a man of character, a true John Bull ; and I myself have not lived nearly thirty years in China without acquiring a considerable experience of the technique of Chinese negotiation. In these circumstances our discussions, carried on in Chinese round a long table in Mr. Ch'en's office, used frequently to last four or five hours on end; when argument would tend to develop into iteration, on the principle of the drop of water wearing away the sandstone rock; and final victory was likely to accrue to the side that went on repeating the same thing long enough.

All Mr. Ch'en's career had been passed in Sinkiang, excepting for some years as Chinese Consul at Tashkent. Speaking Russian fluently, he was no doubt an appropriate instrument for furthering Sino-Russian co-operation in the development of Chinese Turkistan. He had once ridden at the rate of fifty miles a day from Hailar in Manchuria through Outer Mongolia, *via* Urga and Uliasutai, to Urumchi; a remarkable feat of endurance of which one would not have thought so frail a body capable. The Chinese, much as they usually dislike hardship and exercise, have a store of endurance on which to draw when it is absolutely necessary for them to do so.

*   *   *

Our conversations with the Chinese authorities in Urumchi ranged over a wide variety of subjects connected with the political situation in Chinese Turkistan, British trade, the rights and interests of the British Indians in Sinkiang, and all manner of questions connected with the Indian frontier and trans-frontier trade. Our trump card was reference to the precedents and rulings of Nanking, to whose direction in diplomatic questions the Government of Sinkiang professed to bow. The situation in Chinese Turkistan was in many respects curiously anomalous and out of date. Matters of national concern, such as the rate and method of collection of Customs duties on the frontier, passports, and internal taxation, were often administered in vague, irregular and haphazard fashion. Thus the Chinese Customs Administration, that remarkable institution, which for fifty years and more has been the bed-rock of China's finance and foreign trade, has never functioned in Chinese Turkistan, where the local Government collects and disposes of its own customs revenues. The Urumchi authorities did not, however, dispute the principle that China's Customs tariff was one and indivisable and that the dues levied on the Russian and Indian land-frontiers of Chinese Turkistan should be the same as those collected at Shanghai or any Treaty port. Nationality questions were also complicated and troublesome. For there are settled in Sinkiang many British Indians enjoying, as British subjects, exterritorial rights ; whereas the other foreigners in Chinese Turkistan, including Russians, Germans, Afghans, Persians, and an occasional wanderer from Central Europe, Turkey or the Nearer East, were mostly subjected to Chinese jurisdiction. In this way British interests tend to protrude unduly in the body politic of Chinese Turkistan and suffer the resulting friction.

We certainly had no complaint to make as far as assurances of friendship, goodwill and good intentions went. The *Tupan*, *Chu-hsi* and all officials of the Government were profuse with these ; in which respect they were but echoing the feelings of the Central Government ; for the relations between China and Great Britain have never been more cordial than at the present time. The trouble in Sinkiang, where dark, irresponsible and uncontrolled influences have been at work, is to secure the translation of these good intentions into deeds.

* * *

Many dinners and two official banquets were given in our honour, one to welcome us and the other to bid us farewell. The guests included, as well as ourselves, the Soviet Consul-General and his staff and the leading Chinese and Turki personalities. The dinners were served in foreign style, with masses of Russian delicacies and sweet Caucasion wines. Waiters, dressed in white overalls, betrayed only by the bulgings of hidden automatics their military character.

We also " threw a party " in return, mobilizing our joint resources, cooks, orderlies, tinned foods and camp supplies. The Colonel's scarlet-clad Turki *chuprassies* made a gallant show, while my Chinese and Mongol followers donned their best khaki tunics and appeared as waiters for the day.

The speech-making at these festive functions was a tedious business ; for every after-dinner orator had to be rendered in four languages, English, Russian, Turki and Chinese ; and the necessary threefold interpretation, involving prolonged pauses between each sentence, afforded the speaker so much time for the preparation of his next remark that the speeches drifted on interminably.

The Soviet Consul-General also showed us the greatest kindness and hospitality. Monsieur Apresov, an Armenian, had been for some years in the Soviet diplomatic service in Persia and had a good knowledge of Persian and other Central Asian languages. He spoke, however, no English, French, German or Chinese, and most of our intercourse had to be conducted through a Russian-Chinese interpreter.

November 7 is the Soviet National Day. In the course of a long career in China I have assisted at innumerable " joy days " of the nations of the world ;

but never have I seen one so thoroughly celebrated as this Seventh of November in Urumchi. In the morning at 10 a.m. I and Colonel Thomson Glover presented ourselves at the Consulate to offer our congratulations in the customary way. For a couple of hours we sat at a table spread with cakes and sweets while a flow of Turkis, Mongols, Tartars, Russians and Chinese passed through the Consulate reception rooms. In the afternoon we returned at 3 p.m., and, with the *Tupan*, *Chu-hsi* and other notables, sat round the same table, still loaded with the same sweets and cakes, by now more than a little blowzy and dishevelled in the smoke and ashes of innumerable cigarettes. At 4 p.m. we sat down, a company of fifty to a hundred hosts and guests, to a gargantuan feast, the tables loaded with delicious Russian *zakouskas*, fish, caviar, dressed meats, pickles, black bread and butter, off which everyone made a large meal before the real dinner began. The fare was excellent ; and Monsieur Apresov and his staff were charming hosts and showed that the Russians in becoming communists have not lost the art of hospitality and entertaining their guests with the best of food and drink.

The day wore into evening and we became satiated, bemused with food and wine ; while a Buriat dwarf, interpreting the interminable speeches, droned on about the heroes of the Russian Revolution, the benevolent intentions of the Soviet towards the Chinese and Turki peoples, and the friendly feelings of all concerned towards Great Britain in general and myself and Colonel Thomson Glover in particular.

At length about 7 p.m. we rose, some rather unsteadily, from the table and adjourned to the

Consulate cinema, where we were shown pictures of ourselves arriving at the morning's reception, followed by *Chapaev*, one of the masterpieces of Soviet film propaganda, depicting the exploits of a famous peasant leader in the civil wars of the Russian revolution. Unfortunately, whether due to insufficiency of lighting or faulty operation, most of the film was only dimly visible. The Buriat dwarf, interpreting the picture to the Chinese notables, kept up a running commentary about the heroic deeds of the *Hung Tang* (" Reds ") and the villainies of the *Pai Tang* (" Whites ") ; while the distinguished Chinese and Central Asian company dozed and shuffled in their seats. By ten o'clock we were on our way home to bed, having assisted, for nearly twelve consecutive hours, at the celebration of another anniversary of the founding of the Soviet State.

* * *

Urumchi presents many startling contrasts between old and new, a Central Asian city of the Middle Ages provided with electric light, a telephone system, motor-cars and aeroplanes, and wireless communication with the outside world. The original wireless station at Urumchi was erected by the Marconi Company. It was immediately after the Great War that the Chinese Government purchased from the British Marconi Company three high-power wireless stations for erection at Urga, Urumchi and Kashgar, to serve a wireless chain from Peking to the remotest ends of Chinese Central Asia. The transportation across the deserts of Mongolia and Turkistan of this machinery and the enormous wireless masts of steel, and their erection at Urga, Urumchi and Kashgar, constitute one of the epics of engineering history. The Urga station was first to be installed, in 1920 ; but no sooner was it completed and at work than, first the Mad Baron Ungern-Sternburg's raiding Whites, and then the avenging bands of Reds, descended on Mongolia, drove out the Chinese and established a Bolshevik Mongolian State. That was the end, so far as the Chinese Government were concerned, of the Urga station. Those at Urumchi and Kashgar were for a time worked by the local authorities, but both were put out of action, if they were not destroyed, during the Mohammedan rebellion. They were in any case probably rendered out of date by the introduction of more modern wireless methods, which do not need these ponderous iron masts. To complete the sad story of the Marconi stations, the Chinese Government of those days paid for them by the issue of Treasury notes, which, readily taken up on the London market, went almost at once into complete default. Thus did the investing public supply, free of charge, the first wireless stations in Mongolia and Turkistan.[1] The local Government in Urumchi now operate a short-wave station which is in regular communication with China, Russia and Kashgar.

Urumchi also boasts a daily newspaper, the *T'ien Shan Jih Pao* (" Celestial Mountains Daily News "), produced in Chinese by the local Government and purveying to the peoples of Chinese Turkistan such intelligence as it considered proper for their digestion.

[1] The notes were for years quoted at rubbish prices on the Stock Exchange. The present Chinese Government, more mindful than their predecessors of China's financial reputation, are now reported to be taking steps to honour these and other items of China's unsecured indebtedness.

In the evenings after tea Mr. Bien used to read out and translate to us the latest wireless news about the Abyssinian war and other world events. I suppose the news came mostly from Nanking and Russian wireless stations. After it had been taken in by the Urumchi station, edited for the official paper, and finally translated for our benefit by Mr. Bien, the daily budget of news contained at times the most extraordinary items of intelligence, which merely served to whet our appetites for what was really happening in the outside world.

*   *   *

The foreign, non-Russian, community of Urumchi at the time of our visit was very small, the British missionaries, two German Catholic priests and one or two German merchants. The China Inland Mission, the pioneers of Protestant Mission work in China, have long had an establishment in Urumchi under the direction of the veteran Mr. Hunter, who has lived most of his life in Chinese Turkistan and knows more about the country and its peoples than any Englishman. With him were several young men, who, a few years before, had made one of the first journeys from China across the Gobi by motor-truck. Two members of the mission had been carried off by typhus fever while doing devoted work amongst the sick and wounded during the rebellion. The isolation, harsh climate, lack of amenities and unfriendly atmosphere combine to make Urumchi one of the most trying mission stations in the world in which to serve. The courageous little band of men who labour there in the service of the C.I.M. are a devoted company.

There is not much in the way of diversion and

amusement in Urumchi and I had little leisure for making excursions to such places of interest as there may be. The *Tupan*, as part of his generous hospitality, placed at our disposal his Vauxhall saloon, the only car of British make in Chinese Turkistan ; and we were thus enabled to go about, pay our calls and visit the environs of Urumchi in a more elegant conveyance than my motor-trucks. A favourite excursion, for an hour or two between the morning diplomatic wrangle and the evening banquet, was to the public park, below the Red Temple pagoda and across the bridge on the Ili road. Here there was an ornate pavilion, a crude statue of the late Governor of Sinkiang, Yang Tseng-hsin, and pleasure grounds, round which we used to wander, feeding the wild animals, specimens of the T'ien Shan fauna, a bear, wild ass, wapiti, deer, wolves, foxes and the like.

The pleasantest days of our stay in Urumchi were those of our shooting excursions. Sundays were our only free, and therefore shooting, days, when Colonel Thomson Glover and I, taking our guns and a retinue of our respective followers as beaters, sallied forth on to the Dzungarian plain in search of game. We used to drive out a few miles to the neighbourhood of Ku-mu-ti, on the Kuch'eng road, where I had noticed, on my journey in, some likely looking ground. Here we found many partridges and hares and a few pheasants, wild duck and *chikor*. The partridges were the small bearded variety, with black patches on the breast, and afforded good sport, especially when we were able to follow up and separate the coveys, which burst like fireworks when one put them up. On the first Sunday we made in an hour or two a bag of thirty-three of these partridges.

waking them up in the fields and copses and along the hedges, streams and irrigation ditches on the desert's edge. With more local experience, a line of guns and some driving, big bags could readily be made. As a table bird this partridge is delicious, superior to the *chikor*. In places the ground was literally alive with hares, which we had soon to stop shooting, as we could not carry them. We only shot a few pheasants, which were not so numerous ; but we had no dogs. The cocks were big birds of brilliant plumage, resembling those of Northern China. We lunched in hot sunshine in the open ; though there would probably be more than twenty degrees of frost at night. Immediately above us shone the glittering snows of Bogdo Ula. The day's proceedings had the additional charm of the unknown ; for we had no idea, as we pushed on through the pleasant country-side, where we were coming to or what we should find.

* * *

As the days passed and the autumn wore on into winter it became a question whether we should get through our work in Urumchi in time for me to reach Kashgar and cross the Pamir, Karakoram and Himalaya into India before the passes closed. Normally travellers cease to make the journey from the end of October. But it had been done in November ; and Colonel Thomson Glover was of the opinion that, if I started from Kashgar early in December, I should be able to get through. Otherwise it meant waiting until May or June ; since the spring and early summer months are the worst of the year in the Karakoram and Himalaya owing to the deep, soft snow and dangerous avalanches. At last, however, our final interview was over and by the middle of November we were packing up, over-hauling the trucks and making our preparations to take the road again.

CHAPTER VIII

THROUGH EASTERN TURKISTAN : TURFAN, TOKSUN AND KARASHAR

Departure from Urumchi—Tapan Ch'eng—Turfan—
Archæological research in Sinkiang—The Toksun
Gorges—Third breakdown—Truck abandoned at Ku-
mush—Karashar—The Torgut Mongols of Chinese
Turkistan—Difficulties in crossing the Karashar river—
The Russians break the ice.

THE day of our departure from Urumchi dawned at
last. A mantle of white snow carpeted the roofs and
streets and hid the dirt and dust and mud of Sinkiang's
capital. The *Tupan*, Li *Chu-hsi*, General Khoja Niaz,
the Soviet Consul-General, and local notables came
to see us off. We were again an imposing procession
as we rolled out through the Chinese and Moslem
cities, southward bound on the Turfan road. My
two Ford trucks led the way, followed by Colonel
Thomson Glover and his party in two Russian *Amo*
trucks, placed at their disposal by the Provincial
Government ; while the tail was brought up by a
fifth truck containing an escort of soldiers and Mr.
Wan and Mr. Bien, who were to accompany us as
far as Turfan. The effect of our processional departure was, however, soon marred, when one of the
Russian trucks came to a standstill with engine
trouble in the middle of the main street of the Russian
quarter. A stationary motor vehicle that cannot be
induced to move is at the best of times a depressing
and rather humiliating object ; and doubly so when
one comes to a full stop after covering only a mile or

two out of a prospective journey of near a thousand miles. This was the first of many small breakdowns suffered by the *Amo* trucks. After waiting awhile, we went on ahead with the two Fords, feeling our superiority. (But the day was soon to come when the boot would be on the other leg and our old truck, dismembered and disembowelled, left stranded in the desert for good and all.)

Outside the city we entered the hills, through which the road wound for ten to twenty miles. This is the Urumchi gap in the main range of the Celestial Mountains, through which the South Road passes to Turfan and Karashar. Beyond we followed up a desert plain between two ranges, finding the going good, save for some trouble in crossing frozen streams, to reach our stopping-place, Tapan Ch'eng,[1] an old Chinese fort hidden away on the southern face of the T'ien Shan. Somehow or other, without surmounting any pass, we had crossed the watershed of the great barrier range. We had left the Dzungarian plain snow-bound. Here it was very cold, but clear of snow, evidence of the smaller precipitation on the southern side.

We reached Tapan Ch'eng early in the afternoon, having only covered fifty miles or so. The Fords could have made Turfan, another sixty miles. But it was dark before the roaring of engines and grinding of gears announced the arrival of the *Amo* trucks.

Winter had by now descended on Chinese Turkistan. That night my thermometer went down to zero Fahrenheit. From now on we were thankful for our sleeping-bags of Suiyuan sheepskins, tucked into

[1] A hybrid Chinese-Turki name, "The City of the Pass," from the Turki *Dawan*, a mountain pass, and the Chinese *Ch'eng*, a city.

which, oblivious of the smell of greasy, unwashed wool, one could defy the bitterest Central Asian cold. Each morning we had to light fires under the engines of the trucks ; this seemed at first a very dangerous procedure ; but one soon became accustomed to it as part of the routine of winter motor travel.

The next day we crossed the pass, a short, steep climb, testing for the trucks, and descended through the mountains, mostly across bare Gobi, to Turfan. The going was good and the two Fords bowled along across the level desert, each raising the customary cloud of dust, which, in the distance, bore a strange resemblance to the smoke plume of a railway train. *Chikor* partridges were numerous and very tame. A few miles from Turfan, as we were trundling along with the T'ien Shan on our left hand and low Gobi hills on the right, we suddenly, on Serat's direction, turned off right-handed from the main cart road (to avoid, he said, bad sands ahead), and, detouring the hills, emerged on the edge of a giant escarpment, from which we looked down over an infinity of desert far below. Here again, as often in the Gobi, I was reminded of some of the views of the Grand Cañon in the U.S.A. As we descended by a steep and winding trail, my aneroid began to play peculiar tricks, rising to unheard-of barometric heights ; and I realized that we were going down and down, into the famous Turfan depression, the lowest part of which lies nearly one thousand feet below the level of the sea ; a drab desert plain, bounded on the north by the red and yellow hills through which we had descended ; and both hills and plain completely bare and lifeless. Now, in November, it was cold enough, with several degrees of frost at night. But in summer-time the heat in the

Turfan depression is terrific. Passing through an outlying oasis, we ascended again through low dusty hills to reach the famous Turki city of Turfan.

* * *

The oases of the Turfan depression have for centuries been amongst the most favoured and fertile areas of Central Asia. Apart from wars, rebellions and mis-government, life flows in an indolent and easy stream ; a Turki paradise, where the irrigated fields produce unfailingly their heavy crops of corn and cotton, grapes and other Central Asian fruits. Nor is there any fear of excessive or deficient rainfall, floods or droughts, or other visitations. For, while it never rains, the fields are watered by the wonderful system of subterranean irrigation channels, which bring to the dusty land the life-giving water from the mountain depths. All this is a familiar scene in the oases of the dead heart of Asia ; but nowhere is it more impressive than in this neighbourhood, where the surrounding desert is so utterly barren and devoid of every trace of life.[1]

The Turfan depression, lying between the T'ien Shan and a range of desert mountains called the Kuruk Tagh, used to be an ancient Turki kingdom, which lasted down to the time of the Mongol Conquest in the thirteenth century. The ruins of the Uighur capital in the oasis of Kara Khoja not far off are amongst the most famous of the many archæological remains of Turkistan. They have been visited and explored by well-known European orientalists. But the Chinese Government no longer permit foreign archæological research in Sinkiang ; or, rather, they

[1] For description of the underground irrigation system see page 82.

lay down conditions which are generally considered unacceptable by European and American explorers. Recent victims of Chinese jealousy in this respect have been the Hardt-Citroen expedition, Roy Chapman Andrews (in regard to fossil-hunting in Mongolia) and Sir Aurel Stein. Others, including two famous Swedes, Dr. Sven Hedin and Mr. Andersson,[1] got round the difficulty by agreeing to the Chinese terms and working in conjunction with Chinese.

The subject is highly controversial, with charge and counter-charge. In fact both sides to the dispute present a case which has its points. The Chinese complain, and the foreigner cannot well deny, that caravan-loads of priceless treasures from the temples, tombs and ruins of Chinese Turkistan have been carried off to foreign museums and are for ever lost to China. It makes " Young China " boil with indignation to read in the books of foreign travellers descriptions of how they carried off whole libraries of ancient manuscripts, frescoes and relics of early Buddhist culture in Turkistan. And the case of the foreign archæologist is equally or more convincing when they argue that these priceless treasures, if not removed to foreign museums where they can be studied by the most competent of living orientalists, would, as like as not, have been destroyed by Moslem vandals, sold in the bazaars, or left to moulder away to nothing in the desert air. Perhaps the fairest verdict is one of reasonable acquittal of both sides ; holding that, while it may have been right and proper in those early days to remove the treasures to a safer place abroad, further removals cannot nowadays be justified, when the Chinese national conscience is awakened and China at least professes the intention

[1] Author of *Children of the Yellow Earth.*

of herself safeguarding her own archæological treasures from the past.

* * *

We did not see much of Turfan, and nothing of its famous ruins ; arriving early in the afternoon and leaving the next day. We were received by the local military commander, a Chinese from Manchuria, and the magistrate, a Turki (illustrating yet again the new condominium of Chinese-Turki rule), and were most comfortably quartered in a native house. In the late afternoon we all paraded for a ride, myself, Colonel and Mrs. Thomson Glover, the Chinese commandant and Chinese and Turki notables. The city of Turfan, where we were staying, is purely Turkish, native mud houses, covered-in bazaars, mosques, dust and donkeys ; and many Central Asian types, but scarce a Chinese to be seen. A mile or so farther to the east we came to the Chinese city, with Chinese yamens and barracks. All over Turkistan the chief places consist in this way of two cities, the Moslem town and near by a sort of Chinese citadel, generally called the " New City " (in Chinese *Hsin Ch'eng*, in Turki *Yangi Shahr*).

We visited the chief mosques and local sights, including the grape-drying houses, where the seedless raisins, for which Turfan is famous, are dried. The drying process consists of hanging the grapes up in barn-like buildings on the roofs of the houses, with open mud-brick walls ; and the climate does the rest. A small raisin, seedless, sweet and of delicious flavour, is thus produced.

* * *

The next day we had only thirty miles to do to

reach Toksun, a smaller replica of Turfan. But Serat thought he knew better than the guide, and this proved one of the few occasions when his opinion was at fault. As a result we wandered off for another thirty miles across the stony desert to the west, bogged one of the trucks trying to cross an irrigation ditch, and finally had to retrace our steps to rejoin the cart-road, which was very bad, but passable.

At Toksun we were back on the main South Road, from which we had diverged to visit Turfan. We made an early start the next morning ; our minds subdued and anxious ; for Serat, who always took a pessimistic view of things to come, had warned us of the obstacles ahead—the passage of the Toksun gorge, the worst place on the whole route from Peking to Kashgar. In this case his gloomy prognostications proved, unfortunately, only too fully justified.

Our troubles began almost at once, when we broke through the ice of a frozen irrigation ditch just outside Toksun. This was a very minor misfortune, which delayed us perhaps half an hour or so. Yet, reader, imagine your feelings if you met with such an accident in a more normal country—ahead a fair-sized stream of unknown depth, covered by a sheet of ice, say fifteen yards across ; the loaded truck takes it at speed ; crash, in the middle, the rear wheels go through the ice ; and the cumbrous truck is embedded up to the chassis frame in mud and ice ; time 7.30 a.m., sun rising, temperature twenty or more degrees of frost.

Twelve miles from Toksun we entered the mountains by a narrow gorge, with steep precipitous cliffs of bare rock shutting out the sun. The going, in the bed of a frozen stream, was bad. We passed a spring and camping ground, called Arghai Bulak, and reached a little farther on the first of the two bad places, a steep ascent over a sort of landslip or avalanche of rock, where the ravine, narrowing almost to a cleft, was blocked with huge boulders. It seemed impossible to negotiate such a place with loaded motor-trucks, and we worked for some time on the road before making the attempt.

There were two of these boulder-strewn rock land-slides to surmount ; Serat and Chomcha drove each a truck, while the rest of us stood round with picks and crowbars, ready to lend a hand. Both trucks surmounted the first place without incident. At the second the new truck rode triumphantly up the steep incline ; but, as the old one followed and topped the rise, I heard an ominous " crack " in the back axle, which was repeated each time the rear wheels turned a corner or crossed uneven ground.

It was only too apparent that truck *Edsel* [1] had suffered mortal injury somewhere in its interior. We held an engineering council and debated whether we should camp on the spot and take the back axle down. But the place was drear beyond description, barren, gloomy mountains, neither fuel nor water, a day's march from any habitation, and intensely cold. Moreover, the truck could, if driven slowly in a straight direction, still make progress, though the alarming " cracks " continued round corners and on rougher ground ; and fortunately at this very point the gorge opened out into a flat valley, where the going was comparatively good. So we went on, over the pass and down the other side, to reach Kumush, a ruined hamlet, roofless huts and serais, a few stunted trees and dusty, dismal-looking fields. *Edsel*

[1] So named after Mr. Edsel Ford, who had presented it to Dr. Sven Hedin, see page 35.

struggled in, cracking and groaning, and finally subsided, immovable and utterly collapsed, in the middle of the miserable little settlement.

It was by now the afternoon and we set immediately to work to ascertain the damage. Darkness was falling by the time we had removed and opened up the back axle ; a cascade of broken teeth and bits of metal fell to the ground ; the differential gear was smashed to smithereens. The " crack " as the truck rode up the hill announced the breaking off of the first tooth ; and every subsequent " crack " another ; it seemed a miracle that the truck should have reached Kumush in such a state ; the explanation, that, once across the pass, the road had all the way been down an easy slope.

Again I cursed the faulty judgment which had led me to bring *Edsel*, instead of two new trucks. But there was nothing to be done ; we were completely dished, having in our liberal outfit of spare parts no extra differential. The old truck, which had survived two other breakdowns, had now to be abandoned, and may for all I know be lying still in miserable Kumush, propped up on logs and empty petrol drums, disembowelled, back-axle-less.

*　　*　　*

We held a council and soon made our plans. Travelling with Colonel Thomson Glover was a Mr. Raka Ram, an Indian merchant from Kashgar, who, with his baggage and impedimenta, constituted a considerable element in the party of the Consul-General. We decided to leave in Kumush Mr. Raka Ram and his effects, the bulk of my petrol, and four of the Manchurian soldiers who composed our escort from Urumchi ; to proceed with the remaining Ford and Colonel Thomson Glover's Russian trucks to Karashar, only 100 miles away ; and to send back from there a truck to retrieve my petrol and the castaways. Mr. Raka Ram most generously fell in at once with these suggestions ; the soldiers protested vigorously, fearing they were to be abandoned altogether.

The night was very cold, our lodging wretched, and I felt depressed, wishing the journey over and the strain of waiting for the unexpected at an end. Fatal Toksun gorges and miserable Kumush—what unpleasant memories of you I bear away ! The Sinkiang deserts are more sterile and forbidding even than the Gobi and, in all my asiatic wanderings I cannot recall a more depressing resting-place than dirty, ruined Kumush.

The work next morning was depressing, too, unloading the petrol drums, repacking the surviving Ford, and attending to the final obsequies of the abandoned truck. I never really liked old *Edsel*, but now that it was to be left for ever stranded in the deserts of the Kuruk Tagh, I felt I could almost shed a tear over its dismembered corpse.

We also left in Kumush all our superfluous equipment, including the kitchen stove, which we could do without in Sinkiang. But, had we really, the reader may inquire, brought with us 2,000 miles across the deserts of Mongolia and Turkistan a kitchen stove ? Yes ; one of the most valuable items of our camp equipment was a real kitchen stove, made for a few dollars by a Chinese blacksmith in Suiyuan ; and every day, until we got to Hami, it was set up, complete with stove-pipe chimney, in the kitchen tent, where it became the hub round which the camp revolved. We bequeathed our stove and other odds

and ends we had to jettison to the headman of
Kumush.

*   *   *

The Toksun gorges have been the end of many
motor-trucks and cars. Both the Hardt-Citroen
expedition, with their tractors, and Sven Hedin,
with his Fords, got through. The former took ten
hours to do a mile. Dr. Hedin in his book [1] gives a
graphic account of the difficulties his trucks encountered in their passage through the gorge. Sir
F. Younghusband also came this way, in 1887. His
description of the road is still entirely up to date
and the account of his passage through the Toksun
gorge strikes a familiar note. Travelling by cart,
Sir Francis passed the night at Arghai Bulak (" a
spring of clear cold water at the base of a cliff "),
and then spent the whole of the next day, in which
he only covered one and a half miles, in getting his
cart and baggage over the two bad places, where
cliff avalanches had fallen across the gorge and
blocked the road and stream with rocks and boulders.
The place apparently looked much the same fifty
years earlier. [2]

*   *   *

The next day we were up early, working on the
trucks from 6 a.m., in bitter cold ; but it was ten
o'clock before we took the road again. The going all
the way to Karashar was fairly good, over another
easy pass and then, hour after hour, a long and
gradual descent across the sandy desert, with wooded
scrub, elm trees, patches of camel grass and cultiva-

[1] *Big Horse's Flight.*
[2] See *The Heart of a Continent*, by Sir F. Younghusband.

Colonel and Mrs. Thomson Glover Lunching on the Road

The Lower End of the Toksun Gorge

The Rock Passage in the Toksun Gorge : Working on the Road

Truck Emerging from the Rock Passage in the Toksun Gorge

Ladies of Kumush

Headman of Kumush

Street Scene in Karashar

Street Scene in Karashar

tion as we drew near to Karashar. Half-way, on entering Ushak Tal, a fair-sized village, which the Chinese, I know not why, call Ushtala, we had to cross a difficult frozen stream. My heart was in my mouth as our truck, with its heavy extra load of men and goods, crashed through the ice and hung for moments lopsidedly in the stream-bed ; but the powerful V8 engine pulled us safely through. We ate our midday meal in the bazaar at Ushak Tal, its basis Turki rolls, fresh baked, brown, crisp and of delicious flavour. Night was just falling when we sighted the crenellated walls of Karashar ; a good day's run of near one hundred miles.

At Karashar we were back in a Tartar-Mongolian atmosphere. For, unlike all the other towns of Eastern Turkistan, Karashar is not a Turki but a Chinese-Mongol city, being the centre of the Torgut [1] Mongols, inhabiting the T'ien Shan ranges of the hinterland. Lying, with its Mongol population, astride the Great South Road of Eastern Turkistan, Karashar is politically a more important place than its rather down-at-heel appearance would appear to signify. It is also famous for its ponies, reputed the best horseflesh in Turkistan ; and for its mushrooms, which are much sought after by local Chinese gourmets.

* * *

The story of the Torgut (or Kalmuck) Mongols of Sinkiang is one of the great dramas of Central Asian history. They came originally from the steppes of Western Mongolia and Dzungaria and in the middle of the seventeenth century migrated *en masse* into Russia, where they eventually settled down on the

[1] Pronounced *Torrgout*, with French *ou*.

banks of the Volga. A hundred years later they returned to Sinkiang in the circumstances related by De Quincey in his famous essay on *The Revolt of the Tartars*. The Kalmuck Horde on the Volga had come to be regarded as of special value to the military forces of the Russian Tzars and Kalmuck cavalry had played an important part in the defence of Southern Russia against the Moslems. The Russian authorities sought therefore to prevent the return of the Horde to Chinese Turkistan and hundreds of thousands of them perished on the way. What was left of the main Horde reached Sinkiang, where they were well received by the Manchu Emperor of China, who assigned to them the pasturages on which they are still found. Their most important centre is the Karashar neighbourhood, where they spend the summer in the ranges of the T'ien Shan and the winter on the shores of Bagrash Kol.

The history of the Torgut Mongols settled on the Etsin Gol is equally remarkable. This branch of the Torgut tribe left the Volga, while the main Horde were still settled there, to make a tribal pilgrimage to Lhasa. On their return journey they found the way back through Dzungaria blocked by the wars of conquest on which the Manchu Emperors were then engaged. The chiefs of these aberrant Torguts appealed for assistance to the Manchu Emperor, who granted them the grazing grounds on the Etsin Gol where they still reside. These Torguts have therefore been separated from the main tribe for more than two hundred years. Yet they are unquestionably recognized by all Mongols as Torguts and retain the language and customs of the Torgut Horde.

The Torguts of Sinkiang have played but a minor rôle in the stormy politics of the past few years.

They seem to want only to be left alone and to avoid embroilment in the conflict between Moslems and Chinese. Unfortunately they have not been able to keep entirely clear. I do not remember, if I ever knew, the details of the story. But I think the former Governor Chin Shu-jen, hard pressed by Ma Chung-ying, called upon the Torguts to help in the fight against the Moslems. The Torguts refused. The Chinese became suspicious, invited the Torgut chiefs to Urumchi, and had them there assassinated. The present Chinese administration are, I was told, seeking to placate the Torguts, by according to them, as to the Turkis in the rest of Chinese Turkistan, autonomy and a share in the local Government.[1]

*　*　*

We had now reached the second (after the Toksun gorge) of the major obstacles which, as we had been duly warned, lie on the road between Urumchi and Kashgar, namely, the passage of the Karashar river, which flows down, swift, deep and two to three hundred yards in width, from the Celestial Mountains, into a lake, the Bagrash Kol, near by. The question which exercises the mind of every local traveller at this season of the year is the freezing of the river. When the river is open, it is crossed by ferry boat ; when frozen, traffic crosses on the ice ; but for some weeks in spring and autumn, when the ice is breaking up and forming, it cannot be crossed by motor-trucks at all. Serat had told us how on the Sven Hedin expedition they had spent some days in early spring breaking the ice. Now, on the night when we

---

[1] The story of the Torgut Mongols and their present circumstances is well told in *Men and Gods in Mongolia*, by Henning Haslund, a member of Sven Hedin's expedition.

arrived, the river was reported to be open, but forming ice.

Our first preoccupation, however, was to retrieve my petrol and the castaways from Kumush. There were no motor-cars in Karashar, and the Russian drivers of the *Amo* trucks refused to make the double journey back. There was nothing for it but to empty our remaining Ford and send it back. As it was now a race against the freezing river, Serat and Chomcha set off late the same evening. Driving in turns throughout the night they were in Kumush by 6 a.m., loaded the truck, ate and refreshed themselves, and were back again in Karashar before nightfall the next day. This was a wonderful performance on the part of the Ford and the two Mongols, close on three hundred miles in two days and a night ; a record, I am sure, for Chinese Turkistan.

As usual Serat pulled a gloomy face, made the most of all the difficulties—and did the job. But his great effort was in vain. For on the second day, while I was still awaiting his return, Colonel Thomson Glover had taken his two trucks down to the riverside to cross and found the ice already packed and the ferry boats already frozen in. We had " missed the bus " by a single day ; and now, the Chinese said, we should have to wait two to three weeks, according to the weather, before the ice would be thick enough to make it safe to cross with motor-trucks This was another knock-out blow, and meant, it seemed, for me, wintering in Turkistan.

* * *

The river flows just outside the walls of Karashar and was, when I went down to look at it, a sheet of ice, with foot traffic, a stream of Turki peasants and

Street Scene in Karashar

Street Scene in Karashar

Foot Traffic Crossing the Frozen Karashar River

Ferrying the Motor Trucks Across the Frozen Karashar River

their donkeys, already crossing. On the bank a group of Mongol horsemen, who in camp will ride from tent to tent rather than walk a hundred yards, contemplated the scene. In a few days, they said, ponies and camels, and later loaded carts, would cross. Near by a tent had been erected in which was shortly to be held the annual religious ceremony, presided over by the magistrate, to bless, announce or otherwise officially confirm the freezing of the river.

We resigned ourselves to a long wait in Karashar. Our hosts, the *Taot'ai*, a Manchurian, the magistrate, a Chinese official of the old-fashioned type, and other Chinese and Mongol notables, did all they could to make us comfortable and entertained us with the best, mutton and mushrooms, that Karashar could furnish. The local sights and interests were soon exhausted ; one long and dusty street, lined with Central Asian shops, where Mongols, Turkis, Tartars and Chinese jostled one another in the narrow alley-ways.

I had already on arrival telegraphed to Sheng-*Tupan*, asking whether he could lend another truck to help us on our way. Four days later the truck arrived, a new *Amo* in excellent condition, driven by a Russian, who turned out a real good man and more efficient than the majority of Chinese and Russian motor-drivers in Turkistan.

The one thing in which our Chinese hosts expressed their inability to help us was the crossing of the river. With Oriental fatalism they insisted that there was nothing to be done but wait. In any case, they could not really understand the unreasoning impatience of the European always in a hurry.

* * *

But on the fifth day of our stay in Karashar, when we were thinking how to pass the time with shooting expeditions, a God-out-of-the-Machine arrived upon the scene. Serat burst in to bring the news that a party of Russians with three trucks, belonging to the Russian brigade from Aksu or Maralbashi, travelling north, had arrived on the river's southern bank and were at work breaking a channel through the ice! A proposition we had repeatedly pressed our Chinese hosts to undertake and which they had declared impossible. But, to give the Chinese their due, the Russians being on the farther bank, and the ferry boat frozen in on our side, they had the advantage of being able to attach a wire hawser to the heavy barge and drag it, using the engines of their trucks, against the ice, thus greatly facilitating a formidable job.

We all adjourned to the river and interviewed the Russians. They were friendly and invited our co-operation, since our interests were identical, to get the river opened. They wanted our men to help and more particularly that we should induce the Chinese authorities to mobilize a force of local labour.

Soon we were all at work, our men, under the command of Serat, the Russians, and fifty local Turkis recruited by the magistrate. The work was difficult and rather dangerous; as the men had to stand on the edge of the ice and break it up with picks and crowbars; and the stream ran deep and swift. Gradually the clumsy barge was forced through the lengthening channel in the ice; and, the weather being fortunately mild, new ice was slow in forming. By the afternoon of the third day the ferry reached the farther bank. The task was finished, the river open—until the channel froze again!

The first Russian truck got across by half-past two.

Then there was an interlude. Our Russian friends pointed out, politely but firmly, that they had cut the passage through the ice and that a monetary contribution towards expenses would be in order ; and, from the ensuing argument, in Russian, Turki and Chinese, the fact emerged that they were holding up our passage until we paid our way. As the Russians were, nominally at any rate, in Chinese Government employ, and we were travelling under official auspices, we turned them tactfully onto the *Taot'ai* and the magistrate, who, fortunately, were present, entertaining us with tea and cakes and melon seeds on the river-bank. An embarrassing situation for all concerned was liquidated when a bargain was struck at 60,000 *taels* (which sounds a formidable sum but was in reality the equivalent of Chinese dollars thirty-six). This being paid, by the Chinese, the proceedings were resumed.

It took another three hours to get two of our four trucks and the last of the three Russian trucks across ; and each trip coming and going was a nerve-racking affair, getting the truck on and off the ferry and then pushing and pulling the clumsy barge through the channel in the ice. By this time it was after 5 p.m. ; the sun setting behind the Celestial Mountains. The Russians made off, the *Taot'ai* and magistrate disappeared, and with them drifted away most of the men, no doubt forced labour, who had been helping to break and keep the channel open. With the approach of night the cold increased and the ice began to form again. My two trucks, the Ford and the new *Amo*, were still on the wrong side and I knew full well that if they did not cross that night they would remain there until they could be driven over. Somehow or other we got first one and then the other on to the ferry and across ; the second one in darkness. I have seldom felt more relieved than when the last one landed safely on the farther bank. There we found quarters in a Tungan serai. I dreamed that night of loaded trucks plunging through the ice in darkness into the river's depths.

CHAPTER IX

THROUGH EASTERN TURKISTAN : KUCHAR, AKSU AND KASHGAR

Through the heart of Eastern Turkistan—The Konche Darya and the Korla oasis—Kuchar—Kizil—Arrival in Aksu—Fast travelling—Crossing the Aksu river—Heavy sand again—Through the dead forests of the Taklamakan—Arrival in Kashgar—Description of Kashgar— Recent events and present circumstances—The British Consulate—The Russian Consulate and the Swedish Mission—Preparations for departure.

FROM Karashar to Kashgar, a distance of 680 miles, the Great South Road passes through the heart of Eastern Turkistan, traversing a series of rich oases, Korla, Kuchar, Bai, Aksu and Maralbashi, where the big bazaars are packed with Turkis and nowadays a Chinese face is rarely seen. Now that we were clear of Karashar and safely across the river, we still had hopes of reaching Kashgar in time to cross to India before the passes closed ; and we drove from dawn to dusk and sometimes in the dark ; so that there was little time to see the cities and the country-side. It is a region full of interest, with many picturesque and fascinating scenes ; and I regretted having to hurry through at such a pace. The crowds of Turkis thronging the bazaars, with their bearded, pear-shaped, Central Asian faces, a mixture of the Semitic and the Mongol types ; becoming less Tartar and more Persian as one goes farther east ; the men at this season of the year wearing fur caps, poshteens,[1] and, one and all, long leather boots ; the women, in gaily coloured clothes, wearing round hats and white veils wound round the head, their faces in the south heavily veiled, but farther north often not veiled at all ; the traffic on the tree-lined highways through the cultivated lands ; innumerable donkeys, high-wheeled *arba* carts and ponies ; the latter often spilling their riders and careering off across the fields as the trucks drove by ; for the Turki of the cultivated plains, unlike the hill-men, Mongols, Kirghiz and Kazak, are not a race of horsemen. An indolent people (compared with the industrious Chinese), their chief occupation, at least in winter-time, seemed to be eating and sitting in the sun.

Strange that the Chinese should for so many centuries have ruled, and should still rule, this distant alien race ! Unlike Mongolia and Tibet, which have racial and cultural affinities with China, Turkistan seems to have no connection with the Middle Kingdom. But the Turkis are a patient, contented and submissive people, made to be ruled by others. The few that have a knowledge of their rulers' tongue talk Chinese in a high-pitched, plaintive, sing-song tone that I soon learned to recognize—the voices of a subject race. The Kazak and the Kirghiz, on the other hand, descendants of the ancient Huns, have a more virile, warlike mien, and are no doubt less easily controlled. But of the three races playing the chief rôles in the politics of Chinese Central Asia, the Chinese are the rulers born and bred, astute,

[1] The poshteen is the knee-long sheepskin coat of Central Asia, opening down the centre, unlike the Chinese sheepskin robe, a warmer garment, which wraps across the front and fastens, Chinese fashion, at the side.

superior beings, the Tungans the fighters, and the Turkis made by Providence to be the ruled.

* * *

After an early start from Karashar we passed through camel-grass steppe and out into the desert once again. Then we reached a chain of mountains stretching across our front, pierced by a swirling river of clear blue water, which we followed through a winding gorge, with farms, fields full of partridges, a pleasant country-side. Leaving the river, the road emerges from the mountains onto the big Korla oasis, with level desert stretching to infinity beyond.

I was puzzled by the geography of the region through which we passed. Serat explained it. The river we had followed was the Konche Darya, which we had crossed at Karashar, flowing, after its passage through the lake, the Bagrash Kol, into the Tarim, and watering *en route* the Korla oasis. He had been here with Sven Hedin. Korla was the farthest point reached by the latter's expedition on the great South Road. Being prevented by the civil war from going farther on towards Kashgar, they here turned south and east into the Lop Nor country, and thence returned to Kansu ; a remarkable journey to have made with motor-trucks.

We did not enter Korla, but continued west across the desert, with a range of mountains on our right-hand side, passing several small oases, until we reached at nightfall a township called Yangihissar. Here we put up, having made our record journey for the trip, 118 miles in the day.

Now that we were out to cover daily all the ground we could, we drove on each day till nightfall, stopping wherever we might be, generally in serais, which in these towns of Southern Turkistan were better than the serais of the ruined north. And we could make ourselves reasonably comfortable, with rugs and felts spread on the mud *k'ang*,[1] and wood fires burning in the open grates which nearly all the Turki houses have.

The next day we beat our record once again, covering 130 miles to Kizil. After an early start, we made good progress across the level desert and through small oases. By 3 p.m. we had covered more than ninety miles, to Kuchar, the biggest bazaar we had yet seen on the South Road. The streets were so packed with Turki peasants that it was difficult to force a passage with the trucks. Here we were entertained by the Indian *Aksakal*, chief man of the small Indian colony. (The *Aksakal* are Indians, appointed by the Kashgar Consulate, to represent in the scattered towns of Southern Turkistan the interests of the local Indians.)[2] We should have spent the night in Kuchar, where the Turki magistrate had prepared quarters in the yamen for our entertainment. But it was still early in the afternoon, and we decided to continue.

We lost our way in the maze of narrow streets round the bazaar of Kuchar and it was after 4 p.m. by the time we cleared the town. The road turned north-west into the mountains, entering a gloomy gorge. Night overtook us as we wound our way up through a wild and desolate mountain region, and I soon regretted leaving good quarters in Kuchar. We reached the pass, pitch dark and very cold. We

[1] See note on page 89.
[2] *Aksakal* is a Turki word meaning " headman," or, literally, " grey-beard."

In Eastern Turkistan

Women of Eastern Turkistan

Tree-lined Highway in Eastern Turkistan

On the Road in Eastern Turkistan

passed some miserable hovels near the summit and drove on and on, down the mountain on the other side, the winding track illuminated by the headlights of the trucks. At last houses loomed out of the darkness, dogs barking, people's voices. We arrived in Kizil, a bazaar village, and found comfortable lodging.

Near Kizil there are famous cave temples and early Buddhist archæological remains, which have been explored and ransacked by European scholars. But we had no time to visit them, and daybreak saw us on the road again. For the third day in succession we broke our record, covering on this day 139 miles to Aksu. We passed through a succession of oases, watered by the Muzart river, including the town of Bai. We had by now learned to expect bad going in the cultivated lands, owing to the frequent streams and irrigation ditches ; and we were glad when, after sixty miles, the road entered desert hills again, narrow defiles, open desert slopes and sandstone gorges ; with finally a steep descent into the plains at Kara Yulgun. We still had forty miles to do across the desert, and were again benighted, before reaching first Old, and then New Aksu ; where, finding no serai or quarters ready for us, we descended on the *Taot'ai*, a bearded Turki who received his unexpected guests with every courtesy. My camp-bed was set up in the office of the yamen. Our host the *Taot'ai*, stout of figure, rubicund, and wearing a halo of black beard, invited me to dinner, apologizing for the fare, prepared at short notice. I remember that the meal began with a heap of soft-boiled eggs, to be eaten somehow with the fingers. But it was late and I was very hungry and managed quite a few, with well-baked Turki bread and sweet, fresh milk. The

Turki fare is for the European more palatable than wayside Chinese food.

* * *

From Karashar to Aksu we had covered 387 miles in three days. I do not suppose that anyone has travelled at such a pace in Chinese Turkistan before. By this time we had left the two Russian trucks with Colonel Thomson Glover's party far behind. But the *Amo* loaned to me was running well. Its Russian driver seemed to have become infected by our haste and on more than one occasion it was he, rather than Serat or myself, who urged us forward in the dark. Whether because it was a new machine, or because it had a better driver, this truck bowled along with never a hitch, like no other *Amo* we had met in Turkistan.

* * *

At Aksu we had left only 300 miles to reach Kashgar. But on this stretch sand again became an obstacle ; and we ceased to break our daily records and were well satisfied to cover the remaining distance in three days.

We had also one more major obstacle to cross, the Aksu river, which we reached four miles beyond the city walls, flowing in many channels in a stony bed a mile or so in width. We drove through several minor foot-deep channels before we came to the main stream, a green, snow-fed river, swirling along at a tremendous pace. Like the Konche Darya at Karashar, it flows from the glaciers of the T'ien Shan to join the Tarim in the great central desert of Southern Turkistan. There was a bridge, a ramshackle contrivance built for the local ox-carts. It seemed madness to drive a loaded truck across. But we impressed thirty Turkis from some passing carts, built up the bridge and its approaches with planks, stones and faggots, and got the Ford truck safely over. The *Amo* could not climb the rise and had to be unloaded and towed empty up the ramp. Again my heart was in my mouth, as the bridge swayed and trembled under its unaccustomed load. But at last, after three hours' delay, both trucks were landed on the farther side.

By midday we had only covered twenty miles, along a pleasant tree-lined highway through cultivated fields. Then in the afternoon we entered a vast desert and spun along in splendid style ; so that when the sun was going down we had covered nearly eighty miles. In the middle of the desert we drove through an empty town, called Old Chilan, a weird and eerie spot, completely lifeless, the mud houses, mosques and city walls crumbling to dust. Apparently the water supply had failed and the inhabitants had moved out—an epitome of the history of many Central Asian cities.

But the going was too good to last, and in the evening, just as darkness fell, we reached a region of soft sand, amid a forest of dead desert trees. For ten miles we stuck and stuck again. Not since the Gobi had we had such digging, with frequent recourse to all the artifices, with spades and jacks and rope-mats, we had learned to use. At last we reached a village, Yakka Kuduk, where we subsided, tired and hungry, into a serai for the night.

I recall on this day's journey the dust crossing the desert, each truck enveloped in a pall ; the *potai*,[1]

---

[1] The desert roads of Sinkiang are often marked by these ancient beacon towers, called by the natives *potai*, erected at intervals which, I should judge, were intended to represent ten Chinese *li* (three miles). The traveller inquiring the distance of

ancient beacon towers, which lined the track across the desert; and a dead donkey, newly deceased, lying by the road, already partly disembowelled, and two huge vultures sitting by, gorged with meat and guts; in a short space the donkey would be clean skeleton, like the innumerable other skeletons which mark the desert trails of Turkistan.

*　　*　　*

The next day was another hard one, with much spade-work in heavy sand. For hours we toiled through desert forest, where the fine white dust lay ankle and knee deep along the track. We were now skirting the edge of the great central desert of Chinese Turkistan (the Taklamakan), where the atmosphere is shrouded in dust haze and the sun is rarely seen.

At Tumchuk, called Chiu T'ai ("Ninth Stage") by the Chinese, where we lunched off Turki bread, the going for a time improved. Queer rocky mountains, apparently isolated groups, loomed in and out of the dust haze. And so to Maralbashi, bazaar day, and packed with people.

We left Maralbashi with a flying start by a good road at 4 p.m., hoping to do another fifty miles on the way to Kashgar. But ten miles out we were again struggling in heavy sand, threading our way through the dead poplars and clumps of tamarisk.[1]

his journey asks, " How many *potai* to such-and-such a place ? " They served, I suppose, as milestones and beacon towers, for the transmission of news and messages across the desert. The same beacon towers are found on the old highways of Kansu Province, leading to Sinkiang. The Chinese call them *p'ao-t'ai*, " gun-platforms."

[1] Sir Aurel Stein gives the following description of this region of dead and dying forest, the zone surrounding the greatest desert of the world, the Taklamakan, in Southern Turkistan.

" Whether the traveller enters it from the oases, or from the

Kuchar Bazaar

Bai Bazaar

Bridge Over the Aksu River

Towing a Truck on to the Aksu River Bridge : Back View of Serat Direct
Operations

Street Scene in Kashgar

Street Scene in Kashgar

Market Square and Mosque in Kashgar

British Consulate General, Kashgar : December

On Friday morning, November 29, we left the hamlet of Churga in the dark at 5 a.m., determined to cover on that day the 130 miles still separating us from our journey's end, Kashgar. For two hours we drove through the sandy desert in the dark, threading our way through the ghostly forest of dead trees. Then, with the dawn, out into more open country, and on and on across a bleak and dreary desert plain. The road here was very bad, and, in our impatience to get on, we committed the unforgivable offence against the laws of desert motoring by driving too fast over the bumpy ground. With seventy miles to go there was a " crack " and one of the leaves of a front spring had gone ; the first and only mishap to the surviving Ford, which otherwise had not suffered so much as a puncture all the way. We had the spare part, but replacing it would have meant an hour or two's delay ; so we bound the broken leaf with wire and rope and drove on towards Kashgar.

We reached the outskirts of the big Kashgar oasis at Yangi-abad in the middle of the afternoon. From here on the road was good and we bowled along, passing Faisabad, a district city, with only forty miles to go, as the day was drawing in. On and on, soon

jungle belts along the river-beds, he first passes through a zone with desert vegetation, mostly in the shape of tamarisks, wild poplars or reeds, surviving amidst low drift sand. A peculiar feature of this zone consists of the tamarisk cones, hillocks of conical form and often closely packed together. The slow but constant accumulation of drift sand around tamarisk growth has in the course of centuries built them up to heights reaching fifty feet or more. Further out in the Taklamakan there emerge from the dunes only shrivelled and bleached trunks of trees, dead for ages."—*On Ancient Central Asian Tracks*, by Sir Aurel Stein.

in the dark again ; over some doubtful bridges, but in the dark we could not see how bad they were ; with every now and then a " crack " from the front spring, the leaves of which were gradually collapsing. Through Kashgar New City, which is the Chinese citadel, and for a few more miles down a broad high road, until at 7 p.m. we drove up tired and hungry, just as the spring finally collapsed, at the hospitable gates of Chini Bagh [1] outside the walls of old Kashgar.

*　　*　　*

We had travelled the last 680 miles, from Karashar to Kashgar, in six days—good going for motor travel in Chinese Turkistan. The distance, by Ford speedo-meter, from Suiyuan to Kashgar was 2,543 miles. My diary showed that we had covered this distance in thirty-eight travelling days—our shortest daily run eight miles, the longest one hundred and thirty-nine. With proper organization and reasonable luck I would back myself to do the journey from Peking to Kashgar in under thirty days. By camel caravan and cart one would expect to be anything from three to six months on the road.

My surviving Ford truck could claim the distinc-tion of being the first motor vehicle to be driven through from the Chinese border to Kashgar. The next morning we changed the broken spring and a few days later handed it over, washed and brushed up and as good as new, to its new owner, the Consul-General.

*　　*　　*

Urumchi, a Chinese Tartar city of the north, may be—and is—supreme politically in Sinkiang ; but

[1] The local name for the British Consulate-General at Kashgar.

Kashgar is the true capital of Eastern Turkistan ; offering the Asiatic traveller arriving from the bleak and dusty deserts of the north all the attractions of a great metropolis. The shops display a big variety of goods (with, it must be admitted, a preponderance of the products of the Soviet Union) ; the houses, gardens, mosques and fruits are amongst the best in Central Asia ; and living is easy and still marvellously cheap. Above all the atmosphere is friendly and comforting and without the dark and sinister undercurrents that pervade Urumchi. The street scenes in Kashgar Old City are picturesque and colourful, mosques and bazaars, veiled women, Turkis and Central Asian types. The climate seemed to me much the same as that of Northern China and Peking, ranging from zero Fahrenheit in winter-time to 100 in the summer ; the only drawback, the dust haze, which obscures the view and sometimes the sun.

If you look up Kashgar on a Chinese map you will not find it ; but in its place Shu-fu and Shu-lo, which are the names of the Chinese *Hsien*, or districts, administered from Kashgar Old and New Cities respectively. All over Sinkiang the same confusion of Chinese and Turki names prevails. Thus the Turkis call Hami *Kumul* ; and the Chinese always refer to Urumchi as *Tihwa*. It is often a problem for the foreign cartographer to know which name to place upon his map ; for even the smallest hamlets along the post roads have separate Chinese and Turki names.

Kashgar has been through stormy times during the past five years. The story reads like a tale of the *Arabian Nights*, or a nightmare of Turkistan. When the Mohammedan rebellion reached the south of

Sinkiang, all the Moslem races, Turkis, Tungans, Kirghiz and Tajiks, combined to sweep away the thin veneer of Chinese rule. A Turki from Toksun, with the romantic name of Timur, led for a while a native Moslem party, in alliance with the Kirghiz, under one Usman Ali, and the Amirs of Khotan. There was talk of the establishment of an Islamic Republic, based on Kashgar. But Timur was no Yakub Beg. He fell foul of the Kirghiz, chased Usman Ali and his wild hill-men from Kashgar, and was himself, on his way back, attacked and decapitated by Tungan soldiery. This started a new war between Turkis and Tungans. For some months during 1933 the Turkis held and administered in a muddled sort of way Kashgar Old City and the oasis ; while the Tungans, a mere handful in numbers, were besieged in the New City, the Chinese military citadel, a few miles off. The Tungans were outnumbered many times ; but it takes more courage than the average Turki has to tackle a Tungan in his lair, and the Turkis could make no impression on the Tungan stronghold.

Early in 1934 Ma Chung-ying and the main Tungan army, defeated by the Chinese and their Russian allies in the north, arrived in Kashgar, relieved the Tungan force besieged in the New City, drove out the Turkis and set up a Tungan Government.

It was in this fighting between Tungans and Turkis in February, 1934, that the British Consulate was attacked and suffered several casualties, including Mrs. Thomson Glover, who was shot through the shoulder by a Tungan bullet. This unfortunate affair was, however, without political significance ; the Tungan soldiery, ill-disciplined, pursuing the fleeing Turkis, ran amok.

A few months later the victorious army from Urumchi, Russians, Manchurians and Turkis, arrived upon the scene. The Tungans, who could chase Chinese and Turkis round the province, would not face the Russians and retreated without a fight to Khotan and the south ; while Ma Chung-ying himself made terms with the local Russian Consulate and withdrew, a refugee, to Soviet territory. These events brought to a close the Moslem rebellion in Kashgaria.

When we reached Kashgar Chinese rule had long been re-established and was exercised locally by a triumvirate, representing the usual condominium of Chinese-Turki rule ; a Chinese general and *Taot'ai*, both from Manchuria, and a Turki general commanding the Turki troops ; all three outwardly on good terms with one another ; but under tight control from Urumchi. Only a few marches away, holding the southern oases and Khotan, up to the Yarkand river, were the Tungans, under the command of another Ma, General Ma Ho-san, a Kansu relative of Ma Chung-ying.[1] Negotiations for a peaceful settlement were said to be in progress ; but with the Chinese these diplomatic dealings take a long, long time.

I fancy that the Turkis welcomed the return of Chinese rule. Chinese methods are not ours, and Chinese rule in Sinkiang has been freely criticized by foreign travellers in Turkistan, accustomed to other standards. But, by and large, the Chinese mandarins have a genius of their own for colonial administration ; and the Turki peasant probably

---

[1] Most of the leading Moslems of Kansu Province, the home of the Tungans, have for their family name the Chinese character *Ma*, meaning " Horse."

fares better under a Chinese régime than under native Moslem rule.

Of the triumvirate comprising the local Government, General Liu Pin was the Chinese commandant in charge of the Manchurian troops which had reached Kashgar from Urumchi in the summer of 1934. General Liu was somewhat of a local character, raucous of voice from much haranguing of troops, a powerful drinker and a cheery host. Having served in the Manchurian Army in Peking and Shanghai, he was relatively cosmopolitan in his outlook, and had done his best since his arrival in Kashgar to oil the wheels of official intercourse. Mr. Hsü Lien, the *Taot'ai*, another Manchurian, was by contrast quiet and reserved. He had been a professor in one of the Peking universities and lacked the weight and experience of the old-time Chinese mandarin. He seemed rather lost in his strange surroundings. Chinese Turkistan is suffering at present, owing to the strained relations between Urumchi and Nanking, from a lack of experienced officials. The third member of the triumvirate was General Mahmoud, commanding the Turki troops. I recall him as a stout and friendly figure, a merchant or land-owner from Turfan, who had become by force of circumstance a Turki general in the Chinese service.

* * *

At Kashgar my route converged with that followed by Mr. Peter Fleming and Mademoiselle Maillart on their remarkable journey earlier in the same year ; when, coming from the Tsaidam and crossing the Altyn Tagh, they slipped unobtrusively into Southern Sinkiang and passed through the southern oases and Tungan-controlled territory to Kashgar. They saw

Chinese Turkistan mainly through Tungan spectacles. On my journey, on the other hand, I and my party passed through the length and breadth of Sinkiang, but were all the time in Chinese-controlled territory ; and, speaking as we did only Mongol and Chinese, we saw what we observed mainly through Chinese eyes.

* * *

The British Consulate-General at Kashgar, founded many years ago by Sir George Macartney of the Indian Service, is a fine establishment. The Consul-General's house, an imposing building, stands in an ample compound, more like a Legation than a Consulate, housing the offices and staff, a doctor, Chinese and Indian secretaries, Turki orderlies and Hunza scouts. The lay-out is attractive, gardens and terraces overlooking the Kashgar river. Like many other weary Central Asian travellers, we found here rest, hospitality and recreation.

The foreign community comprises the staffs of the British and Russian Consulates and Swedish mission, the colony of Indian merchants, Russians in the service of the Chinese Government, and occasional wanderers from Turkey, Persia, Afghanistan or other country of the nearer East. The isolation is extreme ; I can recall no other British Consulate which is, in time and difficulties of travel, so far away.

The Russian Consul-General, Monsieur Terkulov, an agreeable gentleman of Tartar origin, also maintains a large establishment ; taking, however, second place to his colleague at Urumchi. The Russian Consulate at Kashgar, established under the early Sino-Russian Treaties, ante-dated the British by many years. When the latter appeared upon the scene

keen rivalry prevailed between the two establishments ; the more so in that the Manchu-ruled China
of those days was very sick and her survival far from
certain. Then, after the Bolshevik revolution, the
Russian Consulate disappeared, and the field was for
some years left to the British Consul-General. Since
the re-establishment of the Russian Consulate the
position for the British Representative has not been
easy. For the Russians are geographically at a great
advantage in Chinese Turkistan. British interests in
Sinkiang are best served by the continuance of
Chinese rule ; and British policy has always sought
to work for that end and to oppose the undue growth
of Russian influence. In the days of the Tzars the
Russians pressed hard on Chinese Turkistan. The
new Russia of the Soviet seems also to be exercising
pressure, of a different and more elusive kind, but
none the less effective.

The Swedish Mission, like the China Inland Mission in Urumchi, has an honourable record of many
years of philanthropic, medical and missionary work
to its credit in Kashgar. These are the only two
protestant missionary societies labouring in the infertile soil of Moslem Turkistan. The marches of Mongolia and China are the particular preserve of the
Scandinavian missionaries in Eastern Asia. The
traveller from the Chinese border to Kashgar will,
therefore, as like as not, find a Swedish missionary at
each end of his journey of 3,000 miles. The Scan-
dinavians seem to have a natural affinity for Mongolia
and Turkistan where the names of Larson, Sven
Hedin, Haslund, Norin, Soderbom, and Gunnar
Andersson adorn the records of travel and research.

*   *   *

I arrived in Kashgar on November 29. December 1 had been fixed in my time-table as the latest date on which to leave for India before the route was closed by snow. But the last lap of the journey called for considerable preparations. The trucks could go no farther, and it was necessary to organize a caravan.

Then four or five days after my arrival I fell ill, for the first and only time on the journey. We were entertained to dinner by the local triumvirate, Generals Liu Pin and Mahmoud and Hsü *Taot'ai*; the usual Chinese banquet, with much good food and wine, speeches and Turki music; of all of which I have but a hazy recollection. For after I got home that night I was stricken with a local fever, and spent some days in bed, running a high temperature. I cannot sufficiently express my gratitude to Colonel and Mrs. Thomson Glover, Mr. Barlow, the Vice-Consul, and the doctor for their kind attention.

The fates seemed to conspire against my getting home that winter. But on December 8 the fever left me, and I struggled, weak and wobbly, out of bed, and resumed the interrupted preparations for the road.

The duties of my Mongol-Chinese motor staff had now to be recast. Serat became *caravan-bashi*, leader of the caravan, in which position he acquitted himself as efficiently as in that of head mechanic; Chomcha, master of the horse, and my chief assistant on the march; while Kuo Shu-ming, the Chinese chauffeur, carried on as secretary and accountant of our treasury, consisting now of rupee notes and silver and loads of Kashgar paper money. The latter, to increase the general currency confusion, has an entirely different value to the Urumchi notes.

We hired a caravan of ponies, at the rate of Kashgar taels 2,100 (about Rupees 35) per pony, to take us from Kashgar to Gilgit. The Mongols, Serat and Chomcha, born to the saddle, were quite at home with the Turki ponies. The Chinese rode as Chinese do, making a virtue of necessity. We laid in a stock of Kashgar eatables, overhauled our sheepskins, and bought for each man a pair of snow goggles, a local saddle and a pair of felt-lined Turki boots. None of us could speak the language, and Colonel Thomson Glover was good enough to loan me the services of Hafiz, one of the Turki orderlies from the Consulate, to accompany us as guide and interpreter to Gilgit ; and, culminating kindness, he sent the Consulate doctor with me as far as Tashkurgan in case my fever should return.

CHAPTER X

WINTER JOURNEY ACROSS THE PAMIRS

Routes from Turkistan to India—The Leh and Gilgit
roads—Departure from Kashgar—Old Beeko, the man
from Hunza—Tashmalik—The Ghez Defile—Pamir
lakes—Snow mountains, Kongur and Muztaghata—
Tashkurgan, the farthest Chinese town—Paik and Russianized Tajiks—Hardships and cold—Lopgaz—Crossing the Mintaka Pass—Hindustan at last.

THE main caravan road from Turkistan to India
leads from Yarkand over the Karakoram *via* Leh
to Srinagar in Kashmir. It is one of the most
difficult trade routes in the world, across the desert
ranges of the Kun Lun and Karakoram by passes
sixteen, seventeen and eighteen thousand feet above
the sea, a region of extreme desolation, where
travellers and pack animals die of starvation and
hardship. Nevertheless, a steady dribble of trade
crosses this tremendous mountain barrier during the
summer months.

The alternative route across the Chinese Pamir and
down the Hunza valley to Gilgit is more direct and
is the natural line of communication between India
and Turkistan. The frontier pass on the Gilgit road
is only 15,500 feet above the sea. Owing to scarcity
of supplies and political difficulties, the Gilgit route,
which for some marches runs parallel to and close
by the Russian frontier on the Pamirs, has hitherto
been mainly used as an official road linking the
British Consulate at Kashgar with India. Like
many other Asian trails, it is for hundreds of miles
not so much a road as a direction through the moun-

tains ; until one reaches Hunza, where it becomes a narrow footpath, a foot or so in width, ledged in the mountain-side. It is a month's journey from Kashgar across the Chinese Pamir and Karakoram and down the Hunza valley to Gilgit ; and thence another fortnight's march across the Himalaya to Srinagar and the motor roads and railways of India. But the stages are short, sometimes less than twelve, and seldom over twenty, miles per day.

Both routes are properly open only in the summer and autumn, from May or June to October or November, though the Consulate mail runners manage somehow or other to get through all the year round. We travelled as far as Gilgit in midwinter, arriving there on January 9 ; but it was the coldest journey I have ever made, and beyond Gilgit the passes across the Himalaya on the main road to Srinagar were impassable and blocked by snow.

Such are the roads linking Chinese Turkistan with India. Anyone who has travelled them will realize to the full the physical obstacles which handicap the trans-frontier trade. The Gilgit road, by which we travelled, is the shorter and, I believe, somewhat the less arduous, of the two. But it would require a considerable expenditure to make it and maintain it as a decent track for caravans. The Government of India would no doubt be ready to do something on the Indian section of the road if the Chinese Government would co-operate by doing the same on their side of the frontier pass. But in Chinese-controlled territory trading caravans have from time immemorial been left to find their own way as best they can ; and all over the old Chinese Empire strings of pack animals are year in and year out struggling, slipping and clambering over mountain trails which in other lands would be left to the hunter and the mountaineer.

*   *   *

We left Kashgar on December 9, eight days behind my time-table. I rode a little rat of a Turki pony, selected on account of its ability to amble. The Chinese and most other Asiatics always choose a good ambler for a long journey and I have learned by experience to do the same. However good a pony may be, it is fatiguing day after day to ride an animal that has no pace between a slow walk and a trot. My little Turki mare could trip along at four or five miles an hour and carried me splendidly until she got footsore in the stony Hunza valleys.

We began with three short marches across the Kashgar plain to Tashmalik, a village at the foot of the mountains. It seldom rains or snows in Kashgar, but we always seemed to begin our journeys in unusual weather and it was snowing most of the way to Tashmalik. It was easy travelling, and each night we put up in a good Turki house, with wood fires burning in open grates; the only drawback the absence of windows; or rather windows furnished only with wooden shutters; so that one had to choose between darkness and cold.

We were a large party on the march; myself and my Chinese and Mongols, all of whom I had undertaken to repatriate *via* India; the Turkis in charge of the ponies; the doctor from the Consulate, who accompanied me as far as Tashkurgan; Hafiz, one of the Consulate orderlies; and last but not least old Beeko. The latter had been introduced to me in Kashgar as the Mir of Hunza's representative at Tashkurgan, the Chinese frontier town on the Pamirs.

I had not then grasped his identity or importance. But when I found him riding with me on the road, I learned that he was accompanying me, on the Mir's orders, all the way to Hunza. Beeko was a wizened old man of Hunza, riding a wiry, tireless little hill pony ; he was always at hand when he was wanted, leading the way over the bad places and finding ways and means of surmounting the difficulties and obstacles of the road. His services were invaluable ; and from the day we left Kashgar to that on which we reached Gilgit it was he who arranged all the details of the march and our accommodation and supplies of food and fuel at every stopping-place.

At Tashmalik we entered the mountains by a stony valley, contracting higher up into the Ghez defile and leading from the plains of Turkistan to the plateau country of the Pamirs. (This route by the Ghez defile is only used in winter ; in summer-time it is impassable owing to the depth of water in the stream and a less direct route *via* the Chichiklik pass is followed to Tashkurgan.) The journey now became more arduous, the stages longer and the going worse. A pale sun shone through the snowy mist, but it was very cold : zero at night-time and the maximum fourteen degrees Fahrenheit during the day. The path was one of those aggravating Asiatic trails along a river-bed, endlessly crossing and re-crossing the partly frozen stream. Every crossing was an adventure, as the ponies had to step off the ice on the edge of the stream into the torrent, and stumble, girth-deep, through the racing, icy water amongst the rocks and boulders in the river-bed. The ponies soon became festooned with lumps of ice and our feet and stirrups ice-bound. Some yak we met coming down the road were a mass of tinkling icicles, an extraordinary sight.

It took us all day to cover the twenty-one miles to Tokai, a hut and some rather miserable Kirghiz yurts, surrounded by high craggy mountains looming through the snow and mist. Our luggage was encased in ice and had to be thawed out before we could open up the bags and bedding. This was the first of many cold and cheerless camps.

Then on, the next day, another sixteen miles to Ghez, a group of mud huts and two yurts pitched for our reception, under the shadows of gigantic slopes of rock and snow. Each night while we were on the Pamirs we slept in these Kirghiz yurts, the same round tents of felt, built on a wooden framework, as are used by the Mongols, and in Sinkiang by the Kirghiz and Kazak, from the confines of Manchuria right across Asia to the Kalmuck settlements in European Russia.

From Ghez one enters the long and stony defile, hemmed in by towering walls of rock and snow, which leads up onto the flat, open valleys of the Pamirs. We were warned to prepare for a hard day's journey and made an early start in the dark. Dawn broke and the day wore on as we wound our weary way up through the rocky defile against a bitter wind. At every turn one hoped to see the end ; only to find another reach between the mountain walls where the wind seemed to blow ever colder than in the last. Two ponies fell over a precipice into the stream below ; miraculously, as it seemed to me, no harm was done ; but for the baggage train an hour's delay. In places there were glaciers, and peaks of ice and snow towering above the rocky cliffs ; but the going was too arduous to afford opportunity for enjoyment of the scenery. At last, in the early afternoon, we reached the head of the valley, flatter and more open country, and a lake, called Bulun Kol, backed by snow mountains. Here there was an old Chinese fort, Langt'ai. My spirits rose, until, arriving, we found it ruined and uninhabited, and had to continue for another hour or two to a Kirghiz encampment at the farther end of Bulun Kol.

We got in soon after 5 p.m., having been nearly twelve hours on the road. This march through the Ghez defile in the bitter wind remains in my memory as one of the coldest and hardest day's journey I have ever made. Most of the way I rode my pony wrapped in my Mongol sheepskin robe ; for at that altitude, 12,000 feet above the sea, I found it impossible to walk in all the clothing, woollies, leather waistcoat, coat and sheepskin robe, that I found it necessary to wear. We had to wait another three hours before our baggage train arrived, seated in the Kirghiz yurt and drinking hot bowls of milk, than which nothing could be more comforting.

*　　*　　*

We had now reached the Chinese Pamir, a region of flat valleys resembling the plateau country of Tibet, across which we were to travel, at an average elevation of 12,000 feet above the sea, for another eight marches to the Indian frontier.

I had so often read about the Pamirs that I was glad to have this opportunity of seeing them at last. What traveller, indeed, but would wish to visit once before he dies this far-famed region, the Roof of Asia, where the Hindu Kush, Kun Lun and Karakoram ranges meet and the frontiers of China, India,

Camp at Tokai : The Doctor with the Gun

Camp at Bulun Kol : Early Morning, December 16

On the Shores of Little Karakol Lake : Snows of the Kongur Range in the Background

Telephoto of the Kongur Range (25,000 ft.) from the same Locality

Side View of Muztaghata (24,000 ft.) from near the Pass

Fort at Tashkurgan : Russian Frontier range in the Background

Old Beeko and the Indian Ansakal at Tashkurgan

Photo by Serat and Kuo Shu-ming

Kirghiz Women on the Pamirs

Photo by Serat and Kuo Shu-ming

The Russian Frontier Range, Chinese Pamir, near Yurgul

Camp at Paik

Tajik Headmen on the Chinese Pamir

Group at Mintaka Karaul, Chinese Pamir, December 24 : On the left of the Picture Old Beeko, fourth from the left the Author, fifth from the left Tajik, Officer of Frontier Guards

Lopgaz, the Last Camp in China, 14,000 ft., Christmas Day, 1935

Crossing the Mintaka Pass, 15,500 ft.

Arrival at Gulka-Jawain, the First Camp in India, Boxing Day, 1935:
Author on Yak

The Hunza Karakoram : The First Glimpse of India, from the Foot of
the Frontier Pass

Russia and Afghanistan adjoin ; a region replete
with the romance of Central Asia ; its place-names
conjuring up visions of down-like table-lands, *ovis poli*,
wild hill-men, Kirghiz nomads, Russian intrigues,
cossacks and Chinese mandarins. I found the reality
much like the picture I had formed from books ;
except that the mountains were higher and the
valleys more desolate and barren than I had expected.
But most of the travellers, whose stories I had read,
crossed the Pamirs in the summer and described
green pastures, flowers, and the pleasures of camp
life on these open table-lands. In mid-winter it was
a very different scene, a barren, snow-besprinkled
waste, colder than anything I had yet experienced ;
and biting winds that seemed always to be blowing
in one's face.

For the next ten days, until we crossed the frontier
into India, our main preoccupation was concerned
with fuel. The fuel of the Pamirs is the most unsatisfactory I know. *Argols* (yak dung) are scarce and
one is mainly dependent for firewood on a miserable
sort of desert scrub, which burns, roots and all, like
straw ; so that the fire, lit under the roof-hole in
the centre of the tent, has constantly to be replenished.
It becomes a contest, often unequal, between the
heat and smoke engendered by the fire and the
cold percolating through the roof-hole above one's
head. Outside the tent the thermometer registered
at many of our Pamir camps anything from zero to
twenty degrees or more below. Fuel, fire and cold ;
there was little opportunity in camp to think of anything else ; and it became one's constant care to
see that there was an adequate supply of brushwood
roots and to feed them continuously to the consuming
flames.

Yet even in these unpromising conditions old Liu Kuo-yi, my Chinese cook from Suiyuan, continued to produce his savoury stews of mutton, vegetables and fat ; and these evening meals, and the good Kirghiz milk, were the bright spots to which one looked forward through the cold and weary day.

*   *   *

Leaving Bulun Kol the next morning it was very cold, but the sun shone and the wind mercifully dropped until the afternoon. We travelled fast across the plain, along the shores of lakes ; on our left hand, a huge glittering mass of snow and ice, which from the map I identified as Kongur, whose peaks rise 25,000 feet above the sea. We slept that night at a Kirghiz encampment on the shores of Basi Kol, where I enjoyed the best night's lodging I met with on the Pamirs. Usually we slept in yurts erected specially for our reception and therefore lacking the warmth and comforts of a lived-in dwelling-place. But at Basi Kol I and the doctor lodged in the head-man's tent, well furnished with chests, felts and rugs, where a young Kirghiz tended the fire of brushwood and even added *argols*, and two lambs disported themselves in the corner by the door.

Then we reached mighty Muztaghata, " The Father of Snow Mountains," 24,000 feet in height, an enormous hump of snow blocking the valley's farther end. There were many horns of *ovis poli* lying round, near a camping ground called Subashi, " Head of the Waters," a familiar place-name in Turkistan. A horrible wind got up, bitterly cold, though blowing from the south, which is, it seems, the prevailing wind direction, as the tent openings are generally sited north.

We crossed an easy pass, the first since leaving the plains of Turkistan, across a shoulder of Muztagh-ata. From the summit there were wonderful close-up views of the snows and glaciers of the mighty mountain, which on this side exhibited enormous fissures, as though rent asunder by some gigantic upheaval in the childhood of the world.

That night we spent at Kara Su, below the pass ; a wretched encampment of one Kirghiz family, where we made shift in an uncomfortable camp with an inadequate supply of brushwood fuel. In this as in most of the Pamir camps it was too cold at night-time to undress, while washing was reduced to a minimum or less. Preparations for the night were simple ; letting the brushwood fire go out, drawing the felts across the roof-hole of the tent, and crawling, fully clad, into one's sheepskin sleeping-bag.

From Kara Su we dropped 2,000 feet to Tagarma, where there are cultivated fields, scattered mud houses and a few straggling trees ; and, after a warmer night, or, rather, a night less cold, we followed the Tagarma river through a gorge and reached the Pamir metropolis of Tashkurgan. The Chinese magistrate and a group of wild-looking Tajiks met us on the road and entertained me with tea and mutton in a Kirghiz tent ; and then on to the village, an oasis in the wilderness, where, like other British travellers, we lodged in the mud house of the Aksakal, a venerable Indian, wearing the jubilee medal of His late Majesty King George the Fifth.

*   *   *

Tashkurgan is the administrative capital of the Chinese Pamir region, which we call Sarikol and the Chinese know as P'u-li Hsien ; the last Chinese official centre on the road to India and the most remote magistracy in the whole of the former Chinese Empire. The settlement consists of a village of mud houses, perched on the hill-side above a cultivated plain, and dominated by an old fort, a relic of the Russian occupation before the War. All around are rocky mountains, sprinkled with snow; those on the west being the Russian frontier range. In the past Tashkurgan has at times enjoyed somewhat of a reputation as a storm centre of Central Asian politics. It was here that Safdar Ali, the ruler of Hunza expelled by the Indian Government in 1891, took refuge with the Chinese. Later on the Russians overflowed their frontier and occupied the place with Cossacks. The local situation is now again unsatisfactory; for the Chinese control is weak and the local Tajiks, a race of Aryan mountaineers who inhabit also the neighbouring Soviet Republic of Tajikistan, are under subversive and irresponsible influences from across the border; with the result that British trade and travellers to and from India are subjected to obstructions and annoyances. The solution of this as of many other difficulties in Sinkiang is the restoration of effective Chinese rule. At the time of our visit the Chinese magistrate, an inexperienced youth recently appointed from Urumchi, was in a difficult position, seeming to have little control over his unruly Tajik flock. The circumstances were very different in olden times; when the incumbent of this remote and isolated frontier post would have been qualified by public examination, directly appointed from Peking, and supported by the weight of the official hierarchy of the Chinese Empire.

* * *

The doctor and the escort of Chinese and Turki soldiers from Kashgar now left us to return, while we continued on our way towards the Indian frontier. We left Tashkurgan on December 21 ; and for five days, doing ten to twenty miles a day, we marched up the flat Pamir valleys, gradually ascending, sleeping each night at Kirghiz camping grounds, Yurgul, Dafdar, Paik, Mintaka Karaul and Lopgaz. At each camp we were a little higher than the last, the valley narrower, more snow and ice. On our right hand as we crawled across the Pamir lay the rocky range marking the Soviet frontier. On the farther side, distant only a short day's ride, was the Russian post of Kizil Robat, *fons et origo*, it was said, of the trouble amongst the Tajiks of the Chinese Pamir region. The Russian Cossacks could have walked into Sarikol any day they pleased ; but such crude methods of political penetration are no longer practised by the Soviet successors of the Tzars.

This Pamir trail is a natural line of communication between India and Turkistan. Travelling the way we came, *via* the Ghez defile, there is only one small pass to cross, below the snows of Muztaghata, all the way from Kashgar to the frontier watershed. From Tashkurghan the flat, open valley continues to lead due south ; until, beyond Dafdar, where there are mud houses and a settlement of sorts, it narrows and turns right-handed into the mountains, seeming to pierce the rocky frontier range. Here there was a terrible wind, blowing as always in our faces. Half-way we sheltered in a Kirghiz herdsman's tent, where we refreshed ourselves with good Kirghiz bread and bowls of milk ; a wretched dwelling-place, but it seemed a haven of warmth and comfort after the Pamir wind outside.

At Paik (pronounced to rhyme with *make*), whence another trail leads right-handed across the frontier range to Kizil Robat in Russian territory, there was a post of Tajik soldiers in a stone-built hovel. Farther on, near Mintaka Karaul (another camping ground), we met their commandant, a picturesque and rather rakish-looking figure, dressed in a suit of Russian leather adorned with dangling pistols and ammunition-holders. This gentleman was a well-known local character ; by origin an Afghan, from Wakhan, he had lived many years in Russian territory, and was now working under the Tajik assistant magistrate of Tashkurgan (another dubious character), in co-operation with, if not under the direction of, someone across the border.

The circumstances of the present situation on the Chinese Pamir are too elusive to be properly defined ; due to the ineffectiveness of Chinese rule, and a certain fluidity in the status and nationality of those concerned. For instance, the Russianized Tajik we met at Mintaka Karaul claimed to be a Chinese officer ; a statement which the Chinese authorities alone are in a position to confirm. In appearance he would certainly be taken for a functionary from Tajikistan. In any case, the frontier between the Russian and the Chinese Pamirs is racially an artificial one, with people of the same stock living on either side.

*   *   *

On Christmas Day we made a short march from Mintaka Karaul to Lopgaz, our last camp in China. By this time we had reached an altitude of 14,000 feet or more. The scene was one entirely appropriate to the Roof of Asia, an empty waste of rock and ice, the rounded mountains dwarfed to hills by the elevation of the valley floor, and bitter winds sweeping across the frozen snow. I began to find it increasingly difficult to endure the combination of thin air and cold ; feeling the former most at night-time, when I would wake up panting for breath. At this time of depressed vitality I would conclude that on the wrong side of fifty a man is too old for a winter journey across the Pamir table-lands. Getting up in the morning by candle-light was a grim business too, the smoky brushwood fire raising the temperature inside the tent to the neighbourhood of freezing-point. I was, however, the only member of the party to complain. It was all in the day's work for old Beeko and the Turki pony-men, who spend their lives coming and going across the Pamirs ; for the two Mongols, Serat and Chomcha, camping out in forty or more degrees of frost was nothing new ; and the Chinese, like all Chinese, bore with stoical endurance the hardships which they could not in any case avoid. The ponies, which never had their rugs and saddles off, seemed none the worse for standing out all night in snow and wind.

At Lopgaz we were near the foot of the Mintaka Pass, the frontier between Turkistan and India. The Magistrate of Tashkurgan, instructed by Kash-gar, had kindly caused to be assembled here a mob of yak, to help us cross the pass, so that our ponies could travel empty.

We made an early start on Boxing Day, crawling up the flat valley to the mountain-foot. Wrapped in sheepskins and muffled to the eyes, I sat like a load of baggage on my yak, led by a Kirghiz, his moustache and beard a mass of tiny icicles. Reaching after an hour or two the bottom of the pass, we clambered up, stumbling and slipping over ice and snow. Only the yak could carry loads up such a place. The cold was biting, but mercifully there was little wind. The Mintaka glacier and surrounding peaks loomed through a snowy mist. The angle of my yak altered from the oblique to the horizontal ; we had reached the top. Behind us lay the rounded Pamir hills ; in front a sea of jagged, rocky peaks, the Hunza Karakoram. Standing with old Beeko on the summit of the pass, I saluted Hindustan.

The descent the farther side was very steep, along a glacier ; and then we reached a stone-built hut and camping ground, Gulka-jawain, the first stage in India, where we camped. The Mir of Hunza had been good enough to send supplies of grass and wood to meet us ; so that for the first time for many days the ponies had enough to eat and we sufficient fuel to burn.

The Mintaka Pass is 15,500 feet above the sea. It marks the edge of the Pamir plateau, the knot where the Kun Lun, Hindu Kush and Karakoram ranges meet and the water flows in three directions, down into the basins of the Indus, Oxus and Tarim. There is another way across, the Kilik Pass, a little farther west ; an easier but slightly higher and longer route ; close by the frontiers of Russia and Afghanistan.

The Hunza Road

The Hunza Road

Wedding at Gircha

Wedding at Gircha

CHAPTER XI

THE ROAD TO INDIA

The Hunza road—Murkushi—Misgah—Dangerous cliff
paths—The Batura glacier—Gulmit—The men of
Hunza—*Where Three Empires Meet*—Baltit—The Mir of
Hunza—Connection with China—Baltit to Gilgit—
Stay in Gilgit—Departure of my Mongols and Chinese
by road for Chitral—*Chikor* shooting—Native polo—
The Hardt-Citroen expedition—Flight across the Hima-
laya—Arrival in Delhi.

FROM the Mintaka Pass to Gilgit the road follows
the Hunza river, which flows in a great cleft in the
Karakoram range between huge snow peaks rivalling
in height the giants of the Himalaya and glaciers
which are amongst the biggest in the world. The
track down this tremendous gorge is in keeping with
its surroundings ; a narrow footpath, much of the
way ledged in cliff- or mountain-side, climbing up
and down precipices, fording the racing torrent, and
clambering over rocks and boulders in the bottom
of the gorge. In many places land-slips and rock
avalanches are a constant danger, carrying away the
path and any traveller who may be unfortunate
enough to be upon it at the time.

It is reckoned twelve marches from the pass to
Gilgit ; but the stages are short, usually only three
to four hours' march a day. Many of them could
easily be doubled. But we were getting tired and
glad to have an easy time. Accompanied by Chomcha and old Beeko, and carrying a thermos-full of
coffee and some food in saddle-bags, I used to get
in by midday, or soon after, and enjoy a good meal,

warmed up on the wood fire, while we waited for the baggage train, in charge of Serat and Hafiz, to arrive. Apart from the badness of the road, it was an easy and comfortable journey. At Gulka-jawain, our first stopping-place in India, we were still nearly fourteen thousand feet above the sea ; and in the morning my thermometer registered thirteen degrees below zero Fahrenheit. But this was the last extreme cold we were to experience ; and from now on we had only to walk downhill to Gilgit, with the prospect of reaching lower and warmer stopping-places every day.

*   *   *

The first march was a very short one, dropping steeply down the gorge between peaks of rock and ice, to Murkushi, in a more open valley, with the first trees met since leaving Turkistan. Here the traveller reaches the first of the dak bungalows of India. These rest-houses are, like the road, owned and maintained by the Mir of Hunza. The one at Murkushi, being the last on the road to Turkistan, was primitive enough ; but it had four walls, a fire-place and wood fuel ; and seemed a place of luxury after the draughty tents and brushwood fires of the plateau. I spent the afternoon seated in comfort before a roaring fire absorbed in my first mail, con-taining letters and newspapers forwarded by Major Kirkbride, the Political Agent in Gilgit ; and in the evening feasted on fresh vegetables, bread and Hunza fruits, which the Kirkbrides and the Mir had kindly furnished.

Major Kirkbride, learning of my indisposition at Kashgar, had also been good enough to arrange with the Mir to send a doctor to meet us at Murkushi and escort me down to Gilgit. Sub-Assistant Surgeon

Balbadhar Dar belonged, I think, to the Medical Service of Kashmir, and was seconded for duty as Medical Officer in Hunza ; where his functions and responsibilities covered the widest range, from supervision of the public health of the population of the State to attendance on the ladies of the royal family. Fortunately I did not need to call upon the baboo's services as medical adviser ; but he was helpful in other ways, as well as being an interesting and agreeable companion on the road. A Hindu amongst a tribe of Moslem mountaineers, his point of view was objective and detached ; and his conversation was full of quaint sayings and penetrating observations about the men of Hunza, worthy of being collated as the *obiter dicta* of a " A Baboo in the Wilds."

*   *   *

Another short march down the valley brought us to Misgah, which is the real beginning, or rather end, of the Hunza road, the farthest settlement and cultivation up the river and the end of the Indian telegraph line. Misgah is no doubt pleasant enough in the summer, but in mid-winter it was a rather dreary spot, a few scattered hovels and some stony fields, surrounded by barren mountains and precipices of rock and snow.

At Misgah I learned about my prospects for the journey to the plains of India. The Burzil Pass was definitely snowed up for the season, rendering the Kashmir route impassable. This I had expected, but counted on getting out by the road through Yasin and Chitral ; a long, slow journey, slogging through the snow. I now learned, to my great relief, that the Government of India were most kindly sending an aeroplane to Gilgit to fly me down.

We left our Mongol tents at Misgah since we could now look forward to a rest-house at the end of every march. We had not used them much in Turkistan, or on the Pamirs, where Kirghiz yurts were usually available. But I was sorry to say good-bye to my little felt-lined home, which for so many nights in the Mongolian Gobi had been a snug and comfortable shelter against the wind and cold.

*   *   *

The next stage, from Misgah to Gircha, was the Hunza road at its worst, a footpath, often only eighteen inches wide, shelved in the crumbling cliff. Probably it is in a better state when the Gilgit route to Turkistan is open to travellers during the summer months ; but at this winter season of the year it was in places scarcely passable. We covered the thirteen miles in five hours, having to walk much of the way where the path was too dangerous to ride. Arrived in Gircha, we settled into the rest-house, lit the wood fire and had our midday meal, and sat down to await the arrival of the baggage train. Hour after hour we waited, until finally, after darkness had set in, one of my Chinese arrived and brought news of the caravan ; a pony had fallen from the path and carried away the road where it was shelved in the precipice ; and there had been some hours' delay while the pony and its load were being recovered and the path rebuilt. Overtaken by nightfall, Serat and Hafiz had had to camp with the baggage in the river gorge.

That night I dined with Dr. Balbadhar Dar off Hindu rations, flavoured with the all-pervading ghee ; but hunger is the best of appetizers.

We had to remain a day in Gircha, as it was noon

before the baggage animals arrived. The village was rather a sad little place, typical of Upper Hunza, where the people have a hard struggle to extract a living from the stony and infertile soil, having to eke out with a diet of dried apricots their supplies of corn and meat. But in the afternoon things were enlivened by a village wedding, with music and dancing, which we all went out to watch. Two Mongols, four Chinese, an Englishman, a Hindu, half a dozen Turkis and the local Hunza villagers ; the crowd was truly cosmopolitan.

For the next few days we continued to march down the gorges of the river. Between Kaibar and Pasu we crossed the great Batura glacier, huge masses of dirty, blue-grey ice covered with stones and scree. The track across the glacier was very rough, but I was saved a tiring walk, as the Mir had arranged for me to be provided with a yak, on which I rode triumphantly from shore to shore. The Batura glacier, thirty to forty miles in length and, where we crossed, about a mile in width, is one of the biggest glaciers in the world.

The road now became better, but with many tiring climbs over the cliffs where the passage down the gorge was blocked by precipices. These cliffs, called *paris*, and the narrow, winding paths by which one climbs them, sometimes a thousand feet or more above the river, are a feature of the Hunza road.

Near Gulmit we were met by a young man dressed in " plus fours," with robe and cap of Hunza cloth. He was the Mir's second son, and a keen sportsman, like all the members of his family. He arranged for my benefit a village *tamasha*, music and dancing, of which the men of Hunza, like other Central Asiatics, are very fond. They are an interesting race, of

European rather than Asiatic type. The ruling family claims descent from Alexander. Their clothing is also distinctive, a coarse brown or white homespun, the chief garment the *choga*, a robe-like, long-sleeved dressing-gown, and a round cap, a cross between a beret and a balaclava cap. The men are good horsemen, which is strange, seeing that their country is more suitable for goats than ponies, and polo is their national game. The rest-house at Gulmit was on the polo ground, a long narrow strip between stone walls ; but the winter months are the off-season for the Hunza game.

* * *

On my way down through Hunza I read again that good old book of travel and adventure *Where Three Empires Meet*, a copy of which Major Kirkbride had thoughtfully enclosed in one of my bags of mail. The author, Mr. Knight, was a journalist, who assisted at the Hunza-Nagar war of 1891, when these two little frontier States, whose people up to that time made a living by raiding the Central Asian trade, were brought to book and pacified. After the fighting and the occupation of Baltit, the capital, Knight had accompanied a small column sent in pursuit of Safdar Ali, the ex-Mir, when he fled to Chinese Turkistan. Knight and the column came as far as Misgah, travelling, as we were now doing, in mid-winter ; and he describes the bad places on the road leading up to Misgah just as I found them forty-five years on—crumbling precipices, cliff paths, ponies fording the torrent girth-deep between its banks of ice, and all the rest.

* * *

On January 4 we rode into Baltit, the capital of

Hunza, where there is a well-constructed system of terrace cultivation, irrigation ditches, trees and signs of a better standard of living for the inhabitants. The summer scene in Baltit has often been described, the apricot trees loaded with fruit, running water, greenery and fields of corn ; an oasis in the wilderness, picturesquely dominated by the castle of the Mir. In midwinter the picture was still a striking one, but more austere.

We rested a day in Baltit, enjoying, as so many other travellers have done, the Mir's unbounded hospitality. Sir Muhammad Nazim Khan, K.C.I.E., absolute autocrat of the State of Hunza, ascended the throne after the war of 1891. For five-and-forty years Hunza has enjoyed peace and order under his paternal rule—no small achievement in this distant frontier region. The Mir is remarkably young-looking for his age, and a dignified figure with his auburn beard and gold-rimmed spectacles. He lives the life of a ruler and a country gentleman, in an atmosphere feudal and patriarchal, surrounded by his retainers, sons and grandsons ; of whom I recall the eldest son, Subadar Major Ghazan Khan, a military man of middle age, with red upturned moustaches ; a grandson, Prince Muhammad Jamal Khan, a young man in the twenties, speaking good English ; and one of the Mir's younger sons, a child of three or four. I found some difficulty at first in disentangling the different generations.

The day I spent in Baltit was one of continuous sight-seeing and entertainment, punctuated by meals and long conversations with the Mir, who, drawing on an endless fund of reminiscences, had much of interest to tell about this remote corridor to Central Asia ; from the days of Safdar Ali and his flight to

Turkistan in 1891, to the trans-frontier politics and personalities of the present time. In the afternoon we climbed the hill, the Mir and I mounted on yak, and visited the old fort, the stronghold of the Mirs of Hunza. The situation is most striking, the old castle, built rather in the Tibetan style, backed by a fissured mass of rock and snow and looking down and across the valley to Rakaposhi, one of the giants of the Karakoram. Then we adjourned to the polo ground and witnessed a display of mounted archery ; the riders galloping past and discharging their arrows at a mark, just as the Manchus used to do in olden days.[1] On every appropriate occasion music was provided by the local band, which was usually in attendance close at hand. And in the evening after dinner four dancing boys gave a display of Kabul and Hunza dances, resembling those of Turkistan.

The Chinese used to claim the allegiance of the State of Hunza, as they also claimed as tributaries Burma, Indo-China and Nepal. More than a thousand years ago a Chinese army invaded Hunza from across the Hindu Kush. Traces of the old Chinese connection subsisted until recent days. In the guest-house where I lodged I read the Mir's autobiography, containing many interesting side-lights on local history and the relations between Hunza and the Chinese Empire. As a lad the Mir had visited Kashgar, and he had again crossed the Pamirs when Safdar Ali fled to Turkistan in 1891. The account of the reception of the fugitives by the Chinese officials in Sarikol was a gem of Central Asian history. Nowadays the connection with China is but an echo

---

[1] Every male Manchu had to pass this same mounted archery test before he was entitled to draw his military ration of Chinese tribute rice.

My Mount for Crossing the Batura Glacier

Mounted Archery Sports at Baltit

The Mir of Hunza and Author

The Mir of Hunza, Sons, Grandsons and Retainers

Flight Across the Himalaya : The Start from Gilgit

Flight Across the Himalaya : Haramosh, 24,000 ft.

Over the Himalaya

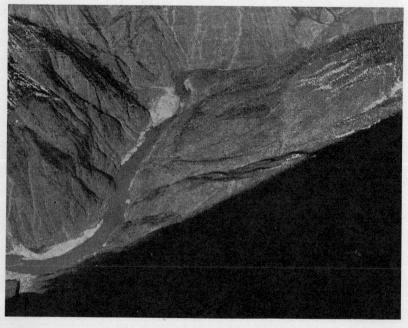

The Gorges of the Indus, from the Air

from the past ; and the men of Hunza and their ruler look alone to India, as they are bound by every canon of geography and race to do.

*   *   *

We left Baltit on January 6, with only four more marches to cover before reaching Gilgit. This lower end of the Hunza road is a fair mule trail, maintained by Government. The journey became daily easier, with, at the end of every march, a comfortable bungalow, furnished with tables, chairs and beds. By now I was getting more than a little weary ; and, easy as the travelling was, I knew no pleasanter moment than the sighting of the rest-house at the end of each day's march. The Hunza torrent, grown to a fair-sized river, was crossed by fine suspension bridges, but still flowed at the bottom of a tremendous gorge, deeper and gloomier than ever, overlooked by great masses of snow and ice. Past Aliabad, where I visited the baboo's hospital ; Nilt, scene of the main assault in the Hunza-Nagar war ; Chalt, where I met the Rajah, ruler of a tiny kingdom, an old gentleman who had played his part in the affair of 1891 ; and Nomal, the last stage before Gilgit, where I made the acquaintance of yet another minor Rajah and found the first green grass we had seen for many weeks. On January 9 the road was good and we had only seventeen more miles to go. Rounding the spur at the junction of the Hunza river with another valley, we met a horseman, Major Kirkbride, who had ridden out to welcome me. An hour later we were crossing the suspension bridge to enter Gilgit. Another lap of the journey was accomplished.

*   *   *

I spent a week in Gilgit, with nothing to do but

enjoy a welcome rest and the hospitality of Major Kirkbride and his charming wife, wait for the aeroplane from India, and make arrangements for my men to travel down by road. There are three routes from Gilgit to the plains ; *via* the Burzil Pass to Srinagar and the motor road to Rawalpindi ; *via* Chilas to Havelian and by rail to Rawalpindi ; and *via* Chitral to the railway at Nowshera. The two former roads were closed by the snow on the passes of the Himalaya ; the latter route, up the Gilgit river and through Yasin and Chitral, a long way round, was reported passable ; and Major Kirkbride had arranged for my men to go that way. None of them could speak any language but Mongol and Chinese. Fortunately there happened to be in Gilgit at this time Colonel Schomberg's servant, Daulat, a cheery and resourceful man of Hunza, who had travelled with his master in Sinkiang [1] and spoke a few words of Turkistan Chinese. Daulat was on his way to join Colonel Schomberg in India, and I was able to engage his services to escort my party down. So off they went, tramping to Chitral through the snow, in charge of Daulat, and armed with chits of recommendation to those in authority *en route*. They had a hard journey, but arrived intact ; and we all met again in three weeks' time in Delhi ; whence I shipped them back to their homes in North China and Mongolia. Thus ended our association, which had begun in Peking four months earlier. They had served me loyally and well ; and to anyone following in my footsteps across Central Asia I could wish no better fortune than that they should be accompanied by Serat, Chomcha and the rest.

* * *

[1] See *Peaks and Plains of Central Asia*, by Colonel Schomberg.

Gilgit is a pleasant spot, with many of the advantages and few of the drawbacks of a frontier post. The men of Hunza, Nagar, and other statelets in the Gilgit Agency, have kept the peace for more than forty years, and there has been no need for military operations here since 1891—a contrast to conditions on the frontier farther west. Gilgit is one of the chief gateways from India to Central Asia. The keys of the gate itself are held by the men of Hunza. Those in authority in India have good reason to be satisfied with the success which has attended a policy of leaving well alone. For those who like the mountains, country sports and nature at her grandest, life in the Gilgit Agency is hard to beat ; its drawbacks, a very small community, almost complete isolation during the winter months, and the height of the surrounding mountains which shut out a good deal of winter sun.

One of the principal diversions in the winter is the local *chikor* partridge shooting, which is well organized by Major Kirkbride and his staff. Many a weary day have I spent on the stony mountain slopes of Northern China chasing the wily *chikor* ; seeking always to get above them ; for otherwise they run and run, invariably uphill, calling derisively to the sportsman panting behind them up the mountain-side. In Gilgit they know better how to deal with the *chikor*, by driving them ; and we stood comfortably in stone-built butts, while the village beaters drove the birds from off the rocky fields and slopes. This was *chikor* shooting *de luxe*, and the birds came fast and high and difficult enough to satisfy the most fastidious.

For those who need more violent exercise there is the native polo, the national game of all this Hunza

Gilgit region. I watched an exhibition match, in which some of the best local players were performing, including two native stars, the Rajah of Punyal and the Mir of Nagar's son. The ground, a long, narrow, dusty strip, was larger and better surfaced but otherwise in principle the same as every Hunza village ground ; instead of boards, a low stone wall, from which the ball, and also the performers, rebounded into play. Six players on each side ; no intervals, the game continuing until one side or the other scores nine goals. The match on this occasion lasted fifty minutes. The players may do practically anything to get the ball and in the way of interfering with the other side. After a goal the game is restarted by the player who scored galloping from the goal-mouth carrying the ball to the middle of the ground, where he tosses the ball into the air and tries to hit it, galloping at full speed, before it falls to earth ; on this occasion only no crossing is allowed ; when it comes off, this air stroke is most spectacular. Another feature of the game is that a player may, if he can, catch the ball with his hand in mid-air and ride off with it towards the other goal, when the game becomes a sort of mounted Rugby football. The sticks are home-made and very whippy, and the stick-work clever ; but the game was rather spoilt by the amount of scrummaging. A band, Hunza style, played throughout the match, *crescendo* as and when a player distinguished himself, especially if he were a Rajah or other eminent personality.

* * *

Gilgit was the farthest point, on the Indian side, reached by the tractor cars of the Hardt-Citroen trans-Asiatic expedition in 1931. Two of the expedition's tractor cars were driven, dragged and carried, in the face of tremendous difficulties and after almost incredible exertions, from Srinagar to Gilgit ; but could, of course, proceed no farther up the Hunza road. The expedition had originally intended driving from Europe across Asia to Peking, passing through Russian and Chinese Turkistan. Political difficulties prevented the execution of this plan. The main body of the expedition came instead through India, and managed somehow or other to get two cars as far as Gilgit ; whence they continued with pack animals through Hunza and across the Pamirs into Chinese Turkistan. At Aksu they met another section of the party, which had crossed the Gobi by motor from the China coast. The two parties, reunited, returned together to Peking.[1] The main body had crossed Asia, but not by tractor car. The gorges of the Karakoram thus defeated, as they will continue in my lifetime to defeat, the attacks of motor-cars. Going the other way, through Russian territory, it should, political obstacles apart, be feasible, with proper preparation, to drive a motor vehicle from Europe across the breadth of Asia to Peking. But I would sooner have for the attempt a good motor-truck of standard make than any patent caterpillar tractor car.

* * *

It was not until I reached Gilgit that I realized to the full how fortunate I was to be flying down to India. Between Gilgit and Rawalpindi lie the ranges of the Western Himalaya, pierced by the impassable gorges of the Indus flowing through independent Kohistan. The R.A.F. have made

[1] See *An Eastern Odyssey*, by Georges Le Fevre.

several flights across the mountains to Gilgit, but always in the summer ; and this was the first occasion on which the flight had been attempted during the winter months. As the date, January 14, fixed for the attempt approached, we watched the weather anxiously. The day was fine, but no aeroplane arrived, and we subsequently learned that the pilot, flying into bad weather in the Himalaya, had been forced back by ice forming on the wings. The next day was fine again, and this time the aeroplane, leaving Rawalpindi about 10 a.m., landed at midday on the Gilgit aerodrome ; accomplishing in two and a half hours a journey that takes from ten to fourteen days by road.

On January 16, my fifty-second birthday, we flew from Gilgit to Delhi. The machine, an Avro, with comfortable cabin accommodation, took off at 10.30 a.m. in perfect weather and climbed immediately to 15,000 feet. The views over the giants of the Kara-koran and Himalaya were dazzling and magnificent, Rakaposhi, Haramosh and Nanga Parbat. We flew over Chilas and down the gorges of the Indus, lying like a great snake at the bottom of a tremendous fissure in the mountains, ten to twelve thousand feet below. The face of the earth was a sea of rugged snow-clad ridges and peaks of rock and ice. Forests began to make their appearance as we got farther over the Himalayan ranges. Here and there were tiny settlements. This was unruly Kohistan, stretching on both sides along the Indus gorges. On the way up a tribal sportsman, holding well forward with his rifle at the swiftly flying mark, had put a bullet through the luggage compartment of the aeroplane. No such adventures befell us going down. The cabin of the Avro was comfortable and warmed ;

and, though we were flying most of the way at over
15,000 feet, I felt no discomfort or ill-effects such as
I had experienced at the same altitude crossing the
Mintaka. But it must have been intensely cold for
pilot and mechanic in the nose of the machine.

About noon we reached the edge of the Himalaya
and saw the Indus flowing out on to the dusty plains
of India. We turned left-handed and slid across the
lower ranges down to Rawalpindi. Lunch in the
Royal Air Force Mess ; and, after some delay in
getting petrol, on again at 3 p.m. The plains of
Northern India seen from the air were very like the
plains of Northern China. We descended at Lahore
for fuel, and on again at 5 p.m., soon in the dark.
Then New Delhi, with its myriad lights, a brilliant
spectacle. We landed in the dark at half-past seven.
The journey, Peking to Delhi overland, was over.
It had taken four months almost to a day.

CHAPTER XII

PAST, PRESENT AND FUTURE IN CHINESE TURKISTAN

Changes and revolutionary ferment in Chinese Turkistan—Recent improvement in the situation—Factors
which have contributed to the restoration of Chinese
rule—Russian influence in Sinkiang—Confused outlook—
Anti-British propaganda—British interests and policy in
Chinese Turkistan—Fascination of the Central Asian
highlands.

CHINESE TURKISTAN was formerly the happy hunting-
ground of big-game hunter, explorer and archæologist. But, with the arrival of inevitable change, it
is no longer so. Gone is the old orderly Sinkiang,
with its venerable Chinese Ambans,[1] peaceful, submissive Turki peasants, and ragged, opium-sodden
Chinese soldiery ; a quiet and attractive backwater
in the stream of human life. And, with the dis-
appearance of the old Sinkiang, gone are the days
of pleasant, easy wanderings in Chinese Turkistan.

The changes in Sinkiang have been evolutionary,
as well as revolutionary. For they are changes
common to the greater part of Asia. Thirty years
ago China, like the Sinkiang of Yang Tseng-hsin,[2]
was an orderly country of dignified mandarins, where
the foreigner (unless he were unfortunate enough to
be killed in a wave of uncontrollable anti-foreign
frenzy) was treated as a superior being, an untouch-

[1] Local Mongol-Turki name for the Chinese magistrates of
Sinkiang ; more commonly known as applied to the Chinese
residents in Tibet and Mongolia under the old Imperial régime.
[2] The Governor of Sinkiang from 1911 to 1928.

able demi-god from another world. Now China is seething with the ferment of awakened Asia, and the Chinese Government and people, struggling to assert themselves against the slights and insults, real and imaginary, of Japan, Europe and America, are chauvinistic, suspicious, jealous and ill at ease.

The new era in China dates from the revolution of 1911 and was accelerated by the Great War which followed that upheaval. But in Sinkiang its arrival was delayed. For seventeen years, from 1911 to 1928, the old Governor Yang Tseng-hsin kept the new ferment out of Chinese Turkistan. When he was killed, in 1928, the changes of the revolution began to take effect in Sinkiang.

Now Chinese Turkistan, like Mother China, is growing up ; and suffering from the ills of adolescence, aggravated, as for a time were those of China, by the Russian influence and inoculation with the serum of the Soviet.

Then, for more than four years, from 1931 to 1935, Sinkiang was ravaged by the Moslem war, a fierce upheaval, in a month of which more blood was shed than in a year of many a Chinese civil war.

It was a life-and-death struggle between Chinese and Tungans ; but the Chinese won out, and at the time of my visit in 1935 there was not a trace of Tungan influence from Hami to Kashgar.

*　　*　　*

Before we left China I had heard on all sides the gloomiest reports of conditions in Chinese Turkistan, where, by all accounts, something like a reign of terror prevailed. In the trading centres on the Chinese border the mere mention of Sinkiang produced head-shakings and gloomy looks. No one in their senses would venture nowadays into that land of ill repute.

We found the picture less black than had been painted. As compared with the chaos of the rebellion years and with the misgovernment of the previous ruler, Chin Shu-jen, the situation at the time of our visit was certainly improved. The civil war was at an end, a measure of law and order, judged by Central Asian standards, had been restored, the main roads were reasonably free from bandits and safe for travellers (safer than those in many parts of China Proper), and the peaceable and ease-loving Turkis were once more growing their corn, melons, grapes and cotton under the protection of Chinese rule. History had thus repeated itself in Central Asia.

Examining the factors which have contributed to this latest come-back of the Chinese in Turkistan, there is, first and foremost, the assistance afforded by the Russians to the Chinese authorities at Urumchi in their struggle with Ma Chung-ying. Without this assistance, the issue would have been at least a doubtful one. The Tungans, that curious Chinese Moslem people, are a race of tough fighters, who have in the past usually dominated the military situation in Chinese Turkistan. But, cut off as they were in Kansu and Sinkiang from supplies of modern war material, they were unable to stand up against the munitions, motor-trucks and aeroplanes furnished to the Chinese authorities at Urumchi from neighbouring Russian territory.

Russian troops also took part in the civil war on the Chinese side ; though whether these troops included regular units from the Soviet Army, I cannot positively say. Dr. Sven Hedin arrived in Korla in 1934 when Ma Chung-ying's Tungan army were in full retreat down the South Road ; and he describes the pursuing troops from Urumchi as being composed mainly of Cossacks.[1] Chin Shu-jen, the predecessor of General Sheng Shih-ts'ai, relied largely on a brigade of White Russian mercenaries, locally re-cruited, for the defence of Urumchi against the Tungans in the early years of the rebellion. This Russian brigade still forms part of General Sheng's forces. But all the Russians in Sinkiang seem now to be under red control. I heard it said that regular Russian troops did take part in the civil war, being euphemistically referred to as *Altai Chün* (" Troops from the Altai "). In any case, whether they were Soviet regulars or not, Russian troops were un-doubtedly the main factor in the defeat of Ma Chung-ying.

The second factor contributing to the success of the Chinese was the timely arrival in Urumchi in the spring of 1933 of the relatively efficient Chinese troops from Manchuria. These troops, expelled by the Japanese from the Three Eastern Provinces, entered Siberia and were transported by arrange-ment between the Chinese and Russian Governments *via* the Siberian Railway to Northern Sinkiang. Relatively well trained and well equipped, they were the first representatives of China's modern armies to enter Sinkiang, and they brought with them into this remote dependency a new spirit of military efficiency and modern ideas. The arrival of these Manchurian troops thus lent a great accession of strength to the Chinese Provincial Government in Urumchi.

The third factor which has contributed to the restoration of the Chinese position has been the

[1] See *Big Horse's Flight*, by Sven Hedin.

attitude of the leaders of the Turkis, who constitute the vast majority of the population of Chinese Turkistan. At the outset the upheaval seemed to take the form of a general Moslem rebellion against Chinese rule. But later on the Tungans and Turkis drifted into conflict (as they were, traditionally, bound to do), the latter went over to the Chinese side, and the struggle assumed rather the character of a civil war between Chinese and Tungans for control of the Province. In 1935, with the situation settling down, the Chinese were definitely embarked on a policy of conciliating the Turkis and co-operating with them in local government. In the old days all the district magistrates and higher civil and military officials were Chinese or Tungans. Now all the magistrates of the Turki districts are Turkis, and several Turki leaders are associated with the Chinese in the Provincial Government ; including notably General Khoja Niaz at Urumchi, General Mahmoud at Kashgar and General Yulbaz in Hami. In official Chinese circles the Turkis are no longer referred to by the local slang expression *Chan-t'ou* ("Turban Heads"), but are known as *Wei-wu-erh* ("Uighurs" —the Turkish race which ruled in Central Asia before the Mongols).

*　　*　　*

The situation in Sinkiang would not be unsatisfactory, from the Chinese point of view, if the National Government of China, and not the Russians, were the power behind the present Chinese rulers in Urumchi. As it is, there is widespread anxiety lest Sinkiang may go the way of Outer Mongolia and become a dependency of the U.S.S.R. Some, including the news organs of Japan, contend that the province has already been overtaken by this fate. The Russians, for their part, disclaim any territorial or political ambitions in Chinese Turkistan. Yet, as apostles of world-wide communism and revolution, their aims in this respect used not to be concealed.

For reasons of geography Sinkiang must, unless special circumstances intervene, be economically dependent on Soviet Russia. The peoples of Chinese and Russian Turkistan are of the same Turki stocks. Compared with the long and arduous routes linking China and India with Urumchi and Kashgar, communications with the neighbouring territories of Russian Central Asia are relatively close and easy. Long before the Great War the Russian manufacturers were paying particular attention to the markets of Central Asia, and an increasing Russian trade with Chinese Turkistan was a natural result of the colonization and development of the neighbouring regions of Siberia and Russian Central Asia. After the Russian revolution relations between Russia and Sinkiang (as between Russia and the rest of China) were broken off and all trade and intercourse were suspended for some years, during which the trade between India and Kashgaria increased and large quantities of Sinkiang produce found their way to China and were exported from Tientsin. In 1924 diplomatic and consular relations between China and Soviet Russia were resumed and trade between Sinkiang and the neighbouring territories of the U.S.S.R. rapidly grew up again. In 1931 the then Chinese Governor of Sinkiang, Chin Shu-jen, concluded with the Soviet authorities a commercial agreement which regularized Soviet state trading in Sinkiang. This agreement was much criticized in China at the time, and, as it was concluded without the authority of the Chinese Central Government, it contributed to the growing estrangement between Urumchi and Nanking. But, in view of the geographical situation of Sinkiang, it was in any case inevitable that the native merchants should send their cotton, wool, skins and meat to the neighbouring Russian markets rather than to the distant coast of China, and that they should turn to the Russian and Siberian manufacturers to supply their needs, especially in bulky and heavy imports such as piece-goods, machinery and iron-ware.

It is therefore only natural that Chinese Turkistan should be dominated economically by the U.S.S.R.; and (as I said in Chapter I) it is inevitable that this economic domination should be accompanied by a measure of political influence, which must rise and fall in accordance with the degree of control exercised over Sinkiang by the National Government of China.

In 1935 Russian influence was strong, indeed overwhelmingly preponderant, in Chinese Turkistan. But the rulers of the province were still Chinese, and far from being communists; and the Chinese connection, if attenuated, still continued to exist. If that connection is ever severed, absorption by the U.S.S.R. will, unless something intervenes, ensue. Turkistan is not likely, at least in our time, to stand on its own legs. China, Russia—or Japan—will take control.

Certainly the picture is dreadfully confused, the outlook blurred. In the North-Western Provinces of China Proper the so-called " red armies," hordes of banditti, with a nucleus of Chinese communists, Moscow's disciples, are still at large; and it is only through these provinces, Shensi, Kansu, Suiyuan and Ninghsia, that the Chinese connection with Sinkiang can be maintained. The Japanese, who claim to be the bulwark against the advancing waves of bolshevism in the Farther East, render confusion worse confounded by the steps they find it necessary in their own interests to take in Inner Mongolia and Northern China. They are busy entrenching themselves on the mainland of Asia against what they regard as the menace of the Soviet. But this involves infringements of Chinese sovereignty, which in turn make it more difficult for the National Government of China to succeed in their stupendous task of reconstructing a modern Chinese State. The future of Sinkiang depends on the results of the efforts they are making to that end.

* * *

During the rebellion absurd reports and stories were published in Shanghai about British intrigues and activities in Chinese Turkistan, where, it was alleged, British agents were busy fomenting rebellion and secession, with a view to the setting up of an independent Moslem State in Turkistan. This kind of nonsense is part of the anti-British propaganda, waves of which well up and die away in the Far East at intervals ; and the Chinese and foreign journalists who write it are habitually provoked into letting their imagination run by any news from Sinkiang, Tibet or Central Asia.

In the case of Chinese Turkistan this trail of propaganda was false from first to last. British policy in Sinkiang, as in China, seeks only peace and trade ; and is, and always has been, patently benevolent to Chinese rule in Turkistan. We regard it as in British interests that the New Dominion should remain Chinese. Sinkiang has always in our experience been Chinese territory; we know and understand the Chinese as neighbours in the East; and any change would almost certainly bring some other Asiatic Power, Russia or Japan, up to the Indian North-West Frontier.

Since the action of the revolution took effect in Sinkiang, British interests, which mean the interests of the Indian residents and those of the trans-frontier trade between India and Turkistan, have suffered and been subjected to pin-pricks and annoyances. This has no doubt been due to the spread in Chinese Turkistan of revolutionary and " anti-Imperialist " propaganda.

Not many years ago in China Proper the Chinese people were taught day in and out that Great Britain was the arch-devil amongst the wicked Imperialistic Powers, who were crushing and devouring the nations of the East. Thanks to the wisdom and patience of those in control of British policy, the Chinese have since learned the truth, which is that one of Britain's fundamental interests in Eastern Asia is to see a strong, stable, prosperous and independent China.

We must similarly be patient with the people of Chinese Turkistan, if they still suspect and misunderstand our motives in their land. The *Tupan* and his Government in Urumchi repeatedly assured us of their goodwill and good intentions. If these were not translated into deeds, and we still had cause to complain of unfair treatment, discrimination, or persecution of British interests in Sinkiang, it would, the *Tupan* said, be due to ignorance and lack of understanding; and, if we would but notify the Government, they would make every effort to set the matter right.

I do not question the sincerity of Sheng *Tupan*

and his colleagues. They wish, while looking first and foremost to their Russian friends for help, to remain on terms of friendship with their Indian neighbour. But they cannot, perhaps they have hitherto not really tried, to control the misguided "anti-Imperialist" enthusiasm of some of their subordinates. And the revolutionary ferment in Chinese Turkistan boils over all the more readily owing to the infusion of intoxicating ideologies from farther west.

British interests in Sinkiang are also particularly vulnerable owing to our being the only representatives of the old "Unequal Treaty" system in Chinese Turkistan. The "Unequal Treaties" would long since have been revised had not external circumstances intervened. It is not the fault of the British Government that they are still in force. When they are finally revised, the going will be easier for all concerned, in China Proper as in Chinese Turkistan.[1]

*   *   *

I have wandered far across the deserts and valleys of Tibet, the marches of North-Western China, Mon-

---

[1] The "Unequal Treaties," of which the Chinese nowadays complain, were concluded between China and the principal foreign Powers in the middle and later half of the nineteenth century. As long ago as 1926 Great Britain declared in favour of Treaty revision, but internal conditions in China and the trouble with Japan have so far delayed the work of revision. Amongst the fundamental provisions of the "Unequal Treaties" is the exterritorial system by which the nationals of the Treaty Powers live in China under the jurisdiction of their own, and outside that of the Chinese, authorities. In Sinkiang, where British Indian subjects may be living amongst, and sometimes partly merged in, the native Turki population, the exterritorial system is bound to produce friction and misunderstanding.

golia and Chinese Turkistan. And this book represents, I fear, my swan song of Asiatic travel; a sad reflection. There is an indescribable charm about the desert lands of Tartary, their sandy plains, fertile oases and rugged mountains; where caravans and stray travellers come and go, bound to and from the remotest ends of Central Asia; and trails of mystery and romance wander off across the far horizon, leading to Peking, Urga, Lhasa and Kashgar. No traveller who has experienced the fascination of the Central Asian highlands but wishes to return; forgetful of the discomforts and monotony of desert travel, the sand and dust, and heat and cold; and mindful only of that mysterious charm that draws the wanderer back to Asia's heart.

APPENDIX

ITINERARY OF THE MOTOR ROUTE FROM PEKING (SUIYUAN) TO KASHGAR

The following itinerary is based on a journey made in September, October and November, 1935, with two Ford V8 motor-trucks from Suiyuan (Kwei-hwa-ch'eng), *via* Hami, Urumchi and Turfan, to Kashgar. It is 1,563 miles *via* Hami to Urumchi (detouring the terminal lakes of the Etsin Gol) ; and 980 miles from Urumchi *via* Turfan to Kashgar ; the total mileage, Suiyuan to Kashgar, being 2,543. The distances in the itinerary are by Ford speedo-meter and the heights by aneroid. While it is possible to start by motor from Peking, the existence of the Peking–Suiyuan railway enables one to begin the motor journey on the edge of the Mongolian plateau, either from Suiyuan or from Kalgan, the two termini of the north-western caravan trade. The best starting-point is Suiyuan, which saves 200 miles as compared with Kalgan. If the start is made from Peking, the Suiyuan route is joined at Pai-ling Miao, ninety-six miles out from Suiyuan and the end of the first stage in the attached itinerary. From Peking to Pai-ling Miao, *via* Kalgan, Chapser and Sunnit, is about 450 miles ; the Nank'ou Pass, thirty-odd miles from Peking, is very bad going for cars ; thence to Kalgan there is a bad cart road ; beyond Kalgan another pass leads up on to the Mongolian plateau ; whence the going is mostly good for the remaining 300 miles across grassy steppe lands to Pai-ling Miao.

* * *

Suiyuan (Kwei-hwa-ch'eng, 3,300 feet) to Pai-ling Miao (Batur Halak, 4,300 feet), ninety-six miles.

Bad going up a stony valley, with finally a steep ascent,

to the top of the first pass fifteen miles from Kweihwa. Then a short steep descent, followed by a long pull up another stony valley, the top of which debouches on to the Mongolian plateau. From here on the trail is a good steppe road, except for a few sandy and muddy patches. At mile 27 reach K'o-cheng (Wu-Ch'uan Hsien), a village where there are Chinese soldiers and passport inspection. At mile 45 reach Chao-ho, a stream which requires careful crossing, a walled fort, and, on rising ground behind, a large monastery. At mile 96 reach Pai-ling Miao (Batur Halak in Mongolian), one of the biggest monasteries in Mongolia. The Monastery lies on a slope backed by low mountains to the south-west and falling away north-east to a stream, on the other side of which is the Chinese bazaar.

* * *

Pai-ling Miao to Uni-ussu (5,000 feet), 164 miles.

A good steppe road for first fifty miles. Soon after reach cultivation and Chinese farms and the road becomes more difficult. At mile 65 one is well in the sandy valley of Yang-Ch'ang-tzu Kou, with much heavy sand. At mile 75 come out on to the undulating steppe again. At mile 105 cross a sandy stream ; care required and bad in wet weather. There is good camping ground on the farther bank above the stream. From here on the grassy steppes of Eastern Mongolia give way to more barren country and the landscape becomes increasingly desert-like as one proceeds west. At mile 110 cross a trail from Pao-t'ou to Outer Mongolia. At mile 122 cross a tussocky plain and pass a monastery a mile or so off the road under the mountains to the south. Indifferent road with patches of heavy sand. At mile 135 reach Hosatu (Chinese Hei-sha-t'u), a group of yurts and huts constituting (in 1935) a Chinese tax station and military post ; junction of roads from Pao-t'ou and Kwei-hwa going north and west. For five miles beyond Hosatu the road runs up a sandy valley with much heavy going. At mile 141, reach the top of the rise and leave the main trail to Shan-tan Miao running west-south-west. From here the road improves with stretches of very good going. At mile 164 reach Uni-ussu, a small stream, yurts of Chinese traders, and (in 1935) a small Chinese military post, the last going west.

Uni-ussu marks the entrance to the desert, though actual Gobi country does not begin until fifty miles or so farther west. The neighbourhood is also the highest point on the road between Suiyuan and Etsin Gol.

Distance from Suiyuan, 260 miles.

* * *

Uni-ussu (Chinese Wu-ni-wu-su) to Hoyer Amatu (Chinese Hai-ya-a-ma-t'u—3,000 feet), 120 miles.

From Uni-ussu the camel trail continues west, but is impassable for motor traffic, and the motor route turns south for ten miles across a tussocky plain to regain the main Shan-tan Miao trail (which cannot be followed on the intervening section owing to a pass through the hills, the Lao-hu K'ou). Road fair. At mile 15 reach edge of plateau with a fine view over an immense stretch of desert to the west, into which the trail descends. At mile 20 and mile 32 are wells and yurts of Chinese traders. At about mile 35 the road starts to cross a belt of sandy desert with many dry stream-beds and other patches of heavy sand. Bad going of this kind for next thirty miles. At mile 50 reach well and Chinese yurts of Sung-Tao-ling, a station of the Sin-sui Company. At mile 55 turn north-west, leaving the main Shan-tan Miao trail running west-south-west. At mile 65 the desert hardens and the going improves. A few miles farther on reach well and yurts of Bayen Unter, under the mountain of that name, which is a prominent landmark from afar. Just beyond Bayen Unter there are bad sand-hills and the motor trail runs either in the dry bed of, or along the edge of, the Meringen Gol, which can be reached by turning south either before or after passing Bayen Unter mountain. Follow the Meringen Gol westwards past the sand hills to about mile 78 and then leave it by turning west-north-west across a gravel Gobi plateau. (In this neighbourhood, at about mile 85, there is a good well of sweet water in a depression off the road to the south.) Continue west-north-west across the gravel desert, good going except after rain, joining at mile 102 an old trail from Teng-K'ou. At mile 105 reach the first of a number of streams, with soft sandy ground in between, very bad in wet weather. On the right hand is Hoyer Amatu mountain, a landmark from afar. Finally, cross high rocky and sandy ground and descend by a better road to Hoyer Amatu, well and yurts, a station of the Sin-sui Company and Chinese trading post, lying in a desert plain bounded on the north by low mountains, which are the border of Outer Mongolia, here only ten to fifteen miles off.

From Suiyuan, 380 miles.

* * *

Hoyer Amatu to Bandin-Tologoi (Chinese P'an-ting-T'ao-lai-Kai, 3,200 feet), ninety-five miles.

Good going to start with, but soon reach much heavy sand. At about mile 25 pass Abter well (Chinese A-pa-tun) in a sandy depression to the south of the road. Soon after leave the camel trail, to avoid bad sand, and turn north-west towards the Outer Mongolian border. At mile 46 pass Yingen well, some five miles off the road to the south, with sweet-water lagoons a mile or so off the road in sand-hills to the north. Yingen well lies at the meeting-point of the frontiers of Outer Mongolia, Suiyuan and Ninghsia, and, according to local Mongols, the detour followed by the Sin-sui trail (in 1935) passes at this point for a few miles through Outer Mongolia. The Outer Mongol patrols re-main, however, in the mountains near by to the north. For the next fifty miles there is much heavy sand, with good stretches of Gobi in between, but soft after wet weather. At mile 57 rejoin the camel trail. At mile 60 there is a sandy depression with difficult heavy pull up out of it on to Gobi plateau. At mile 70 pass a well (Chinese name Ku-lun-pu-shih-Ko). From mile 80 heavy sand, ending with a long heavy pull through low hills. Then a few miles of better going, until one reaches a sandy waste, which has to be crossed to reach Bandin Tologoi, a Chinese trading post and station of the Sin-sui Company ; junction with a road from Ninghsia *via* the Alashan to Outer Mongolia and Urga. All the way on this stage the view is bounded to the north by a low range of mountains, beyond which lies Outer Mongolia with better grass country, these hills marking also the northern edge of the Gobi desert. The well at Bandin Tologoi lies tucked in under the sand-hills west of the yurts ; water not too sweet ; fuel, the usual dead tamarisk, available.

From Suiyuan 475 miles.

* * *

Bandin Tologoi to Wayen Torrai (Chinese Wu-lan-ai-li-ken, 2,800 feet), 154 miles.

Leave Bandin Tologoi by detouring the sand-hills to the north and turn west-south-west across a broad depression. Bad going with patches of heavy sand. At mile 9, below a cliff, there is very soft ground after rain (probably all right in the winter). At mile 18 a well. At about mile 20 start ascending through hills, better road, except for sandy ascents to the low passes in the hills, notably a very steep one at mile 23. At mile 27 a well, off the road to the south. At mile 30 turn north-west and come out on to a plateau, with good road over flat gravel. At mile 38 there is a belt of heavy sand and a well. Thence a fair road again. At mile 51 a double well (sweet water, but no fuel) in the middle of a gravelly plain. The mountains marking the Outer Mongolian border now appear again not far off to the north. Continue west-north-west and enter more hills, good going with sandy patches. At mile 64 reach Deresen Hutuk (Chinese Ch'a-Han-Tien-li-su), a well with yurts of Chinese traders and Sin-sui Company depot. Soon after the hills open out onto a plain, good road. A reddish yellow mountain forms a prominent landmark straight ahead. At about mile 80 the road becomes bad, sandy, stony and intersected by ravines. At mile 88, after passing to the south of the mountain, reach well of Yagan (Chinese Yeh-Kang), no yurts ; there is another small Yagan well farther back under the mountain. At mile 92 enter hills and the road improves, except for steep sandy ascents. At mile 96 reach the top of the range and descend across a gravel plain, very good going. At the bottom there is a belt of sand, with a well (Hao-lai-Kung, no yurts). Indifferent road on, improving as one rises. At mile 121 reach a well, sweet water and fuel, called Kuku Tologoi (" Blue Hillock," Chinese K'o-K'o-T'ao-lai-Kai) from a prominent mound just west of the well. Thence continue west, after detouring to the south-west round some higher hills, good going, with occasional patches of sand. At mile 128 enter hills, at mile 133 come out on to plain, at mile 139 wind through hills again, at mile 145 another plain (bumpy road), and at mile 148 enter last range of hills before descending across a sandy plain to the well of Wayen Torrai, amongst the desert poplars near the east branch of the Etsin Gol (Chinese Erh-li-tzu-Ho). Here there is a Sin-sui depot and (in 1935) a Chinese Government wireless station. After the first few miles out of Bandin Tologoi, the road is fair going, and in places very good, most of the way on this stage.

From Suiyuan, 629 miles.

*   *   *

Wayen Torrai to Ulanchonchi (Chinese Wu-lan-ch'uan-ching, 3,000 feet), round the terminal lakes of the Etsin Gol, 165 miles.

North across a sandy plain, fair going for first dozen miles, with the Etsin Gol sand-dunes on the left. At mile 13 leave the dunes and enter a vast desert of sand and gravel dotted with tamarisk bushes. For the next eighty miles the going is heavy and sandy most of the way, the surface being gravel over sand. At mile 17 Sogo Nor appears, a sheet of blue water a mile or so on one's left. At mile 25 cross salt-encrusted depressions off the lake. At mile 30, continuing north-west, leave Sogo Nor past an *obo* on rising ground.

At mile 65 Gashun Nor appears, a large sheet of water, two or three miles on one's left. At mile 67 enter low hills. A range of mountains run along the northern horizon ; these are in Outer Mongolia, but the actual border is nearer. Continuing to wind through hills, west and north-west, the top of the range is reached at mile 85, with views north-west across to Outer Mongolia and south-west to Gashun Nor, fifteen to twenty miles off. Descend north-west and west and at mile 95 meet and turn south along the Urga-Suchou camel trail, the circuit of the lakes having been completed. From this point on the road is good going for most of the way. Cross a plain and a portion of old lake bottom, excellent road, to reach rising ground at mile 107. Continue through low hills and across undulating desert south and south-east. From mile 125 to 135 the going becomes more sandy, reaching trees and reeds in what appears to be an out-lying oasis of the Etsin Gol. At mile 140 pass a well and at mile 143 a ruined tower amongst sand-dunes. (The Sin-sui trail strikes off south-west from this neighbourhood, without visiting Ulanchonchi.) Then enter tamarisk-dotted desert again. At mile 162 reach junction of the north to south Urga-Suchou camel trail with the east to west China-Sinkiang camel trail (point marked by a tower of dead wood on a sand-hill) and turn east for three miles along latter to reach Ulanchonchi, a mud hut and a yurt comprising a tax station on the west bank of the west branch of the Etsin Gol river. Well water brackish ; river water good when available ; fuel in abundance. Taxes are levied here on goods, brick tea, etc., going from China to Sinkiang and Outer Mongolia.

From Suiyuan, 794 miles.

* * *

Ulanchonchi to Shih-Pan Ching (4,600 feet), 117 miles. A good road across the desert plain west from Ulanchonchi. At mile 3 pass junction with south to north Suchou-Urga camel trail. At mile 20 a sandy patch and well. (The Sin-sui tracks, which do not go to Ulanchonchi, cut-

ting across from the north, join the road near this point.)
At mile 30 more sand. At mile 35 reach well of Lu-Ts'ao
Ching, where there is a depot of the Sin-sui Company in a
mud house. (The water at both this and the previous well
is bitter and there are no more wells until Shih-Pan Ching is
reached.) After Lu-Ts'ao Ching there is another patch of
sand, then good going again. At mile 45 descend into a
depression and ascend between Gobi hills, through which
the road winds for fifteen miles. Fair going. At mile 60
come out onto another big plain. From mile 70 rough
stony going across rising ground. At mile 100, where two
black pyramid hills are a prominent landmark, enter low
Gobi hills and wind through flat valleys, better road,
ascending to reach Shih-Pan Ching, a well tucked away
in the hills, which are marked with upright *obos*, near the
top of the range. Good water. Two yurts of a Sin-sui
Company depot.

From Suiyuan, 911 miles.

* * *

Shih-Pan Ching to Kung-po Ch'uan (5,600 feet) seventy-
nine miles.

Cross the pass almost at once and descend south-west
across a Gobi plain intersected by sandy depressions, in
one of which, at mile 5, there is a well. At mile 10 turn
west, after detouring the range of mountains on the right.
Bad going, sandy and stony, all the way. At mile 16 enter
the mountains, to cross the end of the range. Very heavy
sand. At mile 19, just short of the top of the pass, the camel
trail bears off to the right to the near-by well of Yeh-ma
Ching-tzu (" Well of the Wild Horse "), which is inacces-
cessible to cars owing to a narrow pass. At mile 21 start
descending south-west across a sandy waste, rejoining camel
trail soon after. Better going for a few miles. At mile 31
turn west and north-west to enter the next range of mountains, again very heavy sand. Reach top of the pass at
mile 35 and debouch on to a sloping plateau. Better road.
Continue north-west, crossing at mile 40 an old lake-bottom,

bad in wet weather. Then undulating Gobi steppe, fair road with soft patches, crossing sandy river-bed at mile 52 and gravel hills at mile 56, to reach at mile 67 the well of Huo-shao-ching, in an alkali-covered depression ; fuel available, but very bad water. Continue west by a good road across gravel Gobi to some out-cropping low hills, below which, at mile 79, lies Kung-po Ch'uan, a sweet-water spring, a Sin-sui depot and Kansu tax station (two or three yurts). Junction with a trail south to An-hsi, in Western Kansu, and north to Outer Mongolia. On the hills behind is the ruined fortress of Dja Lama. From Kung-po Ch'uan on the worst of the Gobi is passed, more vegetation, camel herbage and a little tufty grass, begin to appear, and in places there are sweet-water springs (*ch'uan-tzu*) instead of the often bitter desert wells (*ching-tzu*).

From Suiyuan, 990 miles.

* * *

Kung-po Ch'uan to Hami (Kumul, 2,300 feet), 205 miles. From Kung-po Ch'uan the road runs north-west across Gobi plain, with bad going, sand and soft ground, involving many detours, for the first ten miles. Then fair road through low hills and across undulating desert. At mile 20 reach well of Shuang-Ching-tzu. At mile 24 heavy sand. At mile 27 enter the mountains, towards which the road has been heading for some time, passing north of main group, and ascending by steep stony trail to reach at mile 30 the pass, 6,500 feet. (There are wild asses, as well as the usual antelope, in the neighbourhood.) Descend into a plain between two ranges and turn west. At mile 34 there is a spring, Yen-Ch'ih. Good road. At mile 49 enter mountains, which here close in on the plain, by the ruins of an ancient fort and towers, which mark the Sinkiang border, and a mile farther on reach the frontier point of Ming-Shui (1,040 miles from Suiyuan), a ruined hut and spring (sometimes dry) lying in a basin-like plateau in the mountains. Continue north of west through flat valleys. At mile 53 junction with camel trail north-west to Barkul. Fair road, but intersected by dry water runs. At mile 60 another pass, 6,500 feet. (The Ming-Shui plateau and surrounding mountains mark the highest point to which the road has been climbing since leaving the Etsin Gol, and from this pass there is a gradual descent into the plains of Sinkiang.) A sandy valley opens out onto a mountain plain. The snow-clad Karlik Tagh range north of Hami is here seen in the distance to the north-west. At mile 70 there is heavy sand in a dry river-bed for a few miles. At mile 73 reach a sweet-water spring, Wu-t'ung Ta-ch'uan, on the south side of the dry water-course. At mile 74, crossing rising ground, come out on to a vast scrub-dotted desert of gravel, sloping north-west to the base of the Karlik Tagh snow range, now in full view. (The road to Barkul passes to the north of the range.) Continue across this plain, excellent going, reaching at mile 93 a spring and at mile 112 a sandy dry river-bed, the bottom of the slope. From here there is a gradual rise across the desert, direction north of west, round the southern base of the mountains. At mile 115 reach a spring, Wu-t'ung-wo-tzu. The going continues good, until at about mile 139, it becomes stony and inter-sected by dry water runs from the foothills. At mile 145 cross a stream (in October only a few yards wide and a few inches deep) to reach at mile 149 Miao-Erh-Kou (or " Ku "), a small oasis, with trees, under a prominent hill topped by a mosque. In 1935 the farms were mostly in ruins ; a few Turki families. After crossing low hills, continue west across the desert, good road, until at mile 170 sand is reached. Here detour for twenty miles north-west to avoid heavy sand round I-k'o-shu oasis. At mile 190 rejoin camel trail, and enter cultivation. Then a short stretch of desert again, meeting at mile 196 the main cart road and tele-graph line (latter derelict in 1935) from Suchou and Anhsi. At mile 198 enter outskirts of Hami oasis and continue by cart road through cultivated fields to the city of Hami, the centre of which is reached at mile 205.

From Suiyuan, 1,195 miles.

* * *

Hami to Ch'i-chüeh Chingtzu (Ch'i-ku Chingtzu), 115 miles.

Leave Hami oasis after two or three miles. Then good cart road north of west across reed-covered steppe. Small oases, with farms, at mile 18, mile 23, and mile 34 (T'ou P'u, Erh P'u, San P'u—" First, Second and Third Villages "). From San P'u enter desert. Good road, accompanied by telegraph line. At mile 48 reach village of Santao-ling-tzu. On the right hand all the way is the snow-clad Karlik Tagh range, while on the left the ground slopes away into the boundless desert. At mile 61 ruins of a hamlet, and at mile 70 reach the village of Liao-tun. For the next twenty miles the road is rough and stony, rising. At mile 88 reach I-wan Ch'uan (" One Cup Spring "), a ruined posting stage. About here the snow-capped Karlik Tagh range ends and the road enters hills, the beginning of the climb through the gap in the T'ien Shan between the Karlik Tagh and Bogdo Ula ranges. Good road. At mile 99 cross pass to reach Ch'e Ku-lu Ch'uan (" Cart Wheel Spring "), another ruined postage stage. From here descend 2,000 feet by an excellent road for fifteen miles to Ch'i-chüeh Ching-tzu (locally called Ch'i-ku Ching-tzu " The well of the Seven Horns, or Corners "), an old fort in a broad sandy depression between two ranges. Junction of roads to Ku-ch'eng and Turfan.

From Suiyuan, 1,310 miles.

* * *

Ch'i-chüeh Ching-tzu to Ku-ch'eng-tzu (Ch'i-t'ai Hsien, 2,000 feet), 127 miles.

The road to Turfan branches off west into the mountains, that to Ku-ch'eng north-west. Following the latter one enters the mountains at mile 7. The road winds up through a narrow gorge, stony and rocky but not too bad, to reach at mile 20 the ruined posting stage of Ta-shih-t'ou. A mile farther on a low pass (6,700 feet) leads onto a plateau of flat valleys, across which the road runs westwards, good going, for some miles. There is then a gradual descent to open steppe country of poor grass, with the main T'ien Shan range, which has been crossed through the gap above Ta-shih-t'ou, now on the left hand. On the right the steppe slopes away to the horizon. Continue for forty miles across these plains. Good going most of the way. Two more ruined posting stages are passed at mile 43 and mile 62. Ahead is an outlying spur of the T'ien Shan and this is rounded at mile 80 to reach at mile 84 the small walled township of Mu-lei-ho (Mu-li-ho), a district (*hsien*) city. Continue another forty-odd miles, by a good steppe road, gradually descending, to reach at mile 127 Ku-ch'eng-tzu, a large Chinese trading city, terminus of the main camel route from Suiyuan, and seat of a district magistrate. To the south and west stretches the main range of the T'ien Shan, dominated by the peaks of the Bogdo Ula.

From Suiyuan, 1,437 miles.

* * *

Kuch'eng to Urumchi (Ti-hwa, 2,500 feet), 126 miles.

From Ku-ch'eng the road runs at first south-west across the steppe for ten miles towards the peaks of Bogdo Ula, and then, turning west, passes through a series of large oases, with trees, Chinese farms and fields, alternating with stretches of semi-desert steppe. The road is a bad Chinese cart track most of the way, with many streams and irrigation ditches, bridged and unbridged. At mile 22 reach walled district city of Fu-yuan Hsien, and at mile 38 the township of San-t'ai. A mile or two farther on cross a stretch of steppe land over rising ground to reach another oasis and at mile 60 the township of Tzu-ni Ch'uantzu. Again more steppe and then another oasis and at mile 87 the walled district city of Fu-K'ang Hsien. After continuing west across more steppe, at mile 102 turn south to descend through low hills into a cultivated plain. At mile 113 reach village of Kumuti and cross stream. At mile 118 enter more hills, which are crossed to descend to Urumchi, lying in a basin-like valley opening north and backed to the south, south-west and east by the snow-capped peaks of the T'ien Shan.

Distance from Suiyuan, 1,563 miles.

* * *

Urumchi to Turfan (T'u-lu-fan, below sea-level), 114 miles.

Leave Urumchi by the main south road through the Nan-Kuan and continue south through low hills, rough going. After 10 miles meet one of the branches of the Urumchi river and turn east-south-east along a desert plain between two ranges of mountains. Good going for next forty miles. One has here already passed through the Ti-hwa gap between the main T'ien Shan group and their easterly extension the Bogdo Ula range, and the latter is now on one's left hand. At mile 13 reach a ruined inn ; and at mile 30 the village of Ts'ai-o P'u at the head of a small salt lake. At mile 40 cross a small stream flowing south and pass another smaller salt lake. At mile 53 reach small oasis and township of Ta-pan Ch'eng (Da-wan Ch'eng), the only comfortable stopping-place on the way to Turfan. At mile 57 enter the mountains down the gorge of the Ta'pan Ch'eng river flowing south-east and south. Cross stream by a new bridge built for motor traffic, and at mile 58 turn east up a side ravine to ascend to the pass, the top of which is reached at mile 60. Steep ascent and descent, but fair road except for a narrow rocky passage on the pass itself. At mile 62 descend into and rejoin the gorge of the Tapan river. At mile 64 reach a ruined inn and again turn out of the gorge east into low hills, through which the road runs, fair going but narrow in places, for fifteen miles or so. At mile 71 a ruined inn, beyond which the direct road to Toksun branches off south-east. Thence there is a long easy descent, fair road, soft in places, across barren Gobi amongst the hills. At mile 81 reach ruined inn, water and pasturage (San-ko Ch'uan-tze, " Three Springs "). Here the desert opens out onto a plain of gravel, across which the road continues ; fair going all the way with the T'ien Shan range on the left and low hills on the right hand. At mile 99 reach a hamlet and stream, and three miles farther on leave the main cart road and telegraph line to detour the hills to the south (to avoid sand), with a steep descent to and fine views over the Turfan depression. At mile 107 reach a small outlying oasis and at mile 112 ascend to reach at mile 114 the Turki city of Turfan, which lies on the rim above the main depression. For the last few miles the road is a bad, dusty cart track. Turfan consists of two cities, the Turki bazaar and a mile farther east, on the Hami road, the Chinese city, with Yamens and barracks.

* * *

Turfan to Toksun (Chinese T'o-k'o-Sun Hsien, below sea level), thirty miles.

At mile 2 descend to the plain and continue across the desert to reach at mile 7 village and small oasis. Here leave the road from Tapan Ch'eng and turn west-south-west, at first across desert and later a tussocky grass steppe for the rest of the way. At mile 25 reach outskirts of oasis of Toksun. A level cart road, ruts and bad, rough going most of the way.

At Toksun, a small district city and centre of a Turki oasis, one is back on the main south road. The detour to Turfan involves an extra twenty-five miles or so.

Distance from Urumchi *via* Turfan, 144 *miles*.

* * *

Toksun to Karashar (Yen-Ch'i Hsien, 3,300 feet), 152 miles.

Bad cart road through the outskirts of the Toksun oasis for four miles. Then better going, but still rough, across stony desert south towards the mountains, which are entered at mile 12. Bad road up the stream-bed of a narrow winding gorge. At mile 27 reach ruined inn and good water spring of Arghai Bulak, immediately beyond which there are two very bad places where the gorge narrows and the road ascends steeply over rocks and between boulders. (This is the worst place on the road between Urumchi and Kashgar.) After surmounting this rocky passage the gorge opens out into flat valleys and the going improves. At mile 36 reach the top of the pass (5,600 feet), whence there is an easy descent south and south-west through flat and sandy valleys, good going. At mile 40 pass a ruined inn. At mile 48 come out onto open desert, and at mile 57 reach the hamlet of Kumush, with inns. (This is the best half-way place for dividing the stage.) Continue west, good going across level desert, to mile 71, where the road turns south to enter the mountains by another winding gorge, with rather heavy sand in places. At mile 75 there is a ruined inn, where the gorge opens out into a flat valley leading west. At mile 78 cross the pass to come out onto an open desert plateau, across which the road runs westwards, good going, descending gradually. At mile 90 pass another ruined inn and at mile 106 cross stream (no bridge and may be troublesome) to reach the bazaar village of Ushak Tal (Chinese Ushtala) in the cultivated oasis of the river. After crossing more desert reach at mile 115 another oasis with farms and hamlets. From here on the road, good going except for patches of sand, passes alternately through desert, wooded scrub, camel grass plain and cultivation. At mile 128 reach another village, then more desert and strips of cultivation, with many irrigation channels to cross, until Karashar is reached at mile 152.

Once the Toksun gorges are passed the road is good most of the way on this stage. But up to Ushak Tal fuel is very scarce.

Distance from Urumchi *via* Turfan, 296 miles.

* * *

Karashar to Kuchar (3,500 feet), 211 miles.

Going south from Karashar a large river, 200 yards wide, has to be crossed. Motor traffic is ferried over in the spring, summer and autumn, but crosses on the ice in the winter. For some days when the ice is forming and thawing in the early winter (middle of November) and the spring (end of February) it cannot be crossed at all.

On leaving Karashar one has immediately to cross the river, on the farther bank of which there is a village with inns. Thence a rough cart road leads south-west across a camel grass steppe to reach at mile 9 the village of Ssu-Shih-li Ch'eng (" 40 li township "), beyond which one enters sandy desert country. At mile 18 cross rising ground and descend by a better road across sandy desert, to reach at mile 24 a clear swift river at the base of a range of mountains stretching east and west across one's front. The road follows this river (which is the Karashar river after its passage through the Bagrash Kol lake) through the mountains by a picturesque winding valley gorge, with a few farms and much small game. Road fairly good for a mountain trail. At mile 29 reach a barrier with a military post, Ch'ien-Men Kuan. Here the road leaves the river to cut off a corner through the hills, rejoining the valley a mile or two farther on. Immediately afterwards, at mile 31, leave the river flowing south and turn west and south-west to cross low hills, and then descend across a sandy desert to the big Korla oasis, the edge of which is reached at mile 33. The main road does not enter Korla town, which is left a mile or so to the south, but turns west along the edge of the oasis, which lies on one's left hand, with desert and a range of mountains on the right. Good going. At mile 48 reach the bazaar village of Tim. Here the Korla oasis ends (as the stream, the Karashar river, turns off to the south), and the road continues west across desert, sandy in places. At mile 71 reach cultivation and bazaar village, Charchi. Then more desert, in places well wooded, good sandy road. At mile 91 another small oasis and village (Ishma). At mile 98 there is a patch of heavy sand and at mile 101 reach cultivation and bazaar village, Chadir. Between each oasis there is desert and wooded scrub. Fair road. At mile 118 reach bazaar village of Yangi-hissar, the centre of a rather larger oasis and a good half-way halt. From here to Kuchar, ninety-three miles, the road runs alternately

through narrow strips of cultivation and across the intervening stretches of desert, usually bad going in the former,
with many irrigation channels to cross, and fairly good in
the desert. Leaving Yangi-hissar the ground is marshy for
some miles, said to be very bad in wet weather or spring
thaw, but improves as one proceeds. At mile 140 reach
Bugur (Lun-t'ai Hsien), a district city in a larger oasis some
ten miles across, mostly bad going. At mile 157 cross a
stream in the desert and at mile 165 reach a village (Yangi
Abad) in a small oasis with another stream. At mile 176
there is some soft sandy going for a mile or two in the desert
and at mile 178 reach cultivation and another village (Chul
Abad). At mile 193 pass a larger bazaar village (Yakka
Arik). From here on the stretches of desert become less
and trees and cultivation are usually in sight. At mile 202
and 205 cross streams, at mile 206 a sandy stretch, and at
mile 208 enter Kuchar oasis by a broad highway which
leads through suburbs to the town of Kuchar, a district city,
one of the largest bazaars on the south road, approximately
half-way between Urumchi and Kashgar.

Distance from Urumchi, *via* Turfan, 507 miles.

* * *

Kuchar to Aksu New City (3,400 feet), 176 miles.

Leave Kuchar heading north-west for the mountains,
which are entered at mile 6 through a sandy valley, contracting higher up into a narrow gorge. At mile 15 there
is some open valley again, followed by a narrow rocky
defile, which leads by a final steep ascent to the pass reached
at mile 20. Fair road all the way. From the pass there is a
gradual descent westwards by a good road, stony in places,
to reach at mile 37 the bazaar village of Kizil, the first
stopping-place, apart from some miserable hovels, out of
Kuchar. Leaving Kizil, cross stream and continue west
by a rough road through cultivation, to reach at mile 47
a village (Sairam), beyond which there is some heavy sand,
followed by a bad road through cultivation, with sand and
many water channels. At mile 69 reach Bai (Pai-Ch'eng
Hsien), a district city. For the first few miles out of Bai

bad road, crossing streams in stony beds and marshy ground. At mile 76 a stretch of desert, at mile 82 cultivation, at mile 94 cross a river flowing in several streams in a stony bed half a mile wide, two bridges, and at mile 100 reach bazaar village of Yakka Arik. Here the road leaves the cultivated lands to ascend through desert hills, good going. At mile 104 reach pass. Steep descent through a narrow defile and then a good road descending through the hills. At mile 109 a desert inn. Then cross another stretch of desert and at mile 113 enter hills again, followed by another long descent, fair road. At mile 119, continuing descent, enter narrow winding gorge through sandstone mountains. Good road. At mile 122 come out onto a desert plain and at mile 129 start another easy ascent, fair going but sandy. At mile 132 reach the pass, followed by a steep sandy descent into the plain, cultivation and village of Kara Yulgun reached at mile 134. Then a fair road across sandy desert, ascending, heavy in places. At mile 141 reach top of the rise, then better going across level descert, crossing sandy streams at miles 141, 142 and 145. Heavy sand approaching bazaar village of Jam, reached at mile 147. Cross a river, two bridges. Then bad road through cultivation, sandy, and many water channels, for some miles, improving after mile 160. At mile 167 steep descent to and ascent from a stream-bed and at mile 168 reach Aksu Old City (District City of Wen-su Hsien). Descend by a good road, to reach at mile 176 Aksu New City (A-K'o-su Hsien), now a separate district city.

On this stage the road is fair to Kizil (37 miles), bad thence to Yakka Arik (mile 100), fair thence to Kara Yulgun (mile 134), bad thence to mile 160, and better for the rest of the way.

Distance from Urumchi, *via* Turfan, 683 miles.

* * *

Aksu to Maralbashi (Pa-chu Hsien, 3,300 feet), 147 miles.

Leave Aksu, New City, going south and cross branch of river, bridged, immediately outside the town. At mile 4 reach the Aksu river, flowing in several channels in a bed a mile wide. Ford subsidiary channels (in November a foot or so deep) and cross main stream by bridges under construction in 1935, very bad, not fit for motor traffic. (There is also a ferry which furnishes a safer and speedier way of crossing the river.) Continue south and south-west for thirty miles through cultivated land, road much of the way a broad tree-lined highway, bad going in places and slow throughout owing to many water channels. At mile 10 a hamlet, and at mile 18 cross large river by several good bridges, followed by some marshy ground through paddy fields. At mile 20 small bazaar village, beyond which there is bad sand. At mile 25 and 31 small bazaar villages. At mile 32 cultivation ends and the road enters sandy desert. For the next forty miles the going is fair and fast in places, but there is heavy sand at miles 35–36, 57–58, and 69–70. At miles 39 and 47 desert inns, at mile 59 an empty ruined town (Old Chilan), and at miles 73 and 82 more desert inns. From mile 75 there are twenty-odd miles of bad sand. At mile 86 reach small bazaar village of Yakka Kuduk (Chinese Shih T'ai, " Tenth Stage "). At mile 93 a hamlet. By mile 96 the worst of the sand is over and the going improves. At mile 97 another desert hamlet, and at mile 103 enter cultivated land, farms and fair road. At mile 112 reach bazaar village of Tumchuk (Chinese Chiu T'ai, " Ninth Stage "). Then more cultivated land with patches of desert, fair road. Beyond mile 122, after leaving a hamlet and turning west round base of low mountains, the road is bad for a few miles across a steppe of reedy grass. At mile 130 reach bazaar village of Charbagh (Chinese Pa T'ai, " Eighth Stage "), beyond which the road is slow and bumpy again across desert. At mile 137 reach fields and farms and continue by fair road for the rest of the way to Maralbashi.

On this stage the road is slow for thirty miles, fast for the next forty-five miles, bad sand for the next twenty miles, and mixed fair to bad the rest of the way.

Distance from Urumchi, *via* Turfan, 830 miles.

* * *

Maralbashi to Kashgar Old City (4,000 feet), 150 miles.
Leave Maralbashi by a good road and at mile 5 enter
desert. From mile 10 heavy sand for twenty miles. At
mile 18 small bazaar village of Churga. At mile 30 miserable desert inn. At mile 37 reach some cultivation and
small bazaar village (Tungan Mazar). Then more heavy
sand, especially at mile 41. At mile 42 more cultivation
with better road, and at mile 47 reach bazaar village of
Urdiklik. Thence for the next forty miles the road is very
bad and bumpy across a dreary desert. Miserable desert
inns or hamlets at miles 64, 69 and 74. At mile 90 the
desert ends and at mile 91 reach village of Yangi-abad.
From here, except for some patches of marshy ground, the
road is good, mostly through oasis country with bridges
over the streams, for the rest of the way to Kashgar. At
mile 104 reach Faizabad (Chia-shih Hsien), district city,
at mile 111 a small bazaar village, at mile 126 bazaar village
of Yaman Yar, at mile 134 another bazaar village, at mile
144 Kashgar New City, and at mile 150 the British Consulate-General outside Kashgar Old City.

The road on this stage is bad for ninety miles, in places
very bad, and good for the last sixty miles.

Distances from Urumchi, *via* Turfan, 980 miles.

INDEX

C. W. HARRISON
Illustrated Guide to the
Federated Malay States
(1923)

BARBARA HARRISSON
Orang-Utan

TOM HARRISSON
World Within: A Borneo
Story

CHARLES HOSE
The Field-Book of a
Jungle-Wallah

EMILY INNES
The Chersonese with the
Gilding Off

W. SOMERSET MAUGHAM
Ah King and Other Stories*

W SOMERSET MAUGHAM
The Casuarina Tree*

MARY McMINNIES
The Flying Fox*

ROBERT PAYNE
The White Rajahs of Sarawak

OWEN RUTTER
The Pirate Wind

ROBERT W. SHELFORD
A Naturalist in Borneo

CARVETH WELLS
Six Years in the Malay Jungle

SINGAPORE

RUSSELL GRENFELL
Main Fleet to Singapore

R. W. E. HARPER AND
HARRY MILLER
Singapore Mutiny

JANET LIM
Sold for Silver

G. M. REITH
Handbook to Singapore
(1907)

C. E. WURTZBURG
Raffles of the Eastern Isles

THAILAND

CARL BOCK
Temples and Elephants

REGINALD CAMPBELL
Teak-Wallah

MALCOLM SMITH
A Physician at the Court of
Siam

ERNEST YOUNG
The Kingdom of the Yellow
Robe

Titles marked with an asterisk have restricted rights.